Young Believer Case Files

Compiled by Stephen Arterburn with Carol and Gary Wilde

Stephen Arterburn
with Carol and Gary Wilde

Tyndale House Publishers, Inc.
Wheaton, IL

Young Believer™

CASE FILES

Visit Tyndale's exciting Web site at www.tyndale.com

Compiled by Stephen Arterburn
Edited by Erin Keeley
Designed by Jacqueline L. Noe

Published in association with the literary agency of Alive Communications, Inc., 7680 Goddard Street, Suite 200, Colorado Springs, CO 80920.

Library of Congress Cataloging-in-Publication Data

Arterburn, Stephen, date.
Young believer case files : true stories of young believers / by Steve Arterburn ; with Carol & Gary Wilde.
p. cm.
Summary: A collection of more than two dozen true stories of teens living out their Christian faith, each of which is followed by a suggestion to read a particular Bible passage and questions to think about.
ISBN 0-8423-6199-5
1. Christian children—Religious life—Juvenile literature. 2. Christian life—Juvenile literature. [1. Christian life. 2. Conduct of life.] I. Wilde, Carol. II. Wilde, Gary. III. Title.
BV4571.3 .A78 2003
248.8'3—dc21 2003009959

Printed in the United States of America

08 07 06 05 04 03
6 5 4 3 2 1

Contents

1. Sudden Storm 1
2. Out of Control 7
3. Needing Help—But What Kind? 11
4. The Chase 15
5. Love, Hate, and Tears 21
6. Toughest Job You'll Ever Love 25
7. Keeping the Faith in Hard Times 29
8. Safety Pins and Postmen 33
9. Brock's Prayer 39
10. Breana's Brave Battle 43
11. Help, One Cookie at a Time 47
12. My Friend Sammy—Still the Same 53
13. He Will Fill You 57
14. From Promise to Fulfillment 61
15. Now You're Cooking! 65
16. When Belief Just Stops 69
17. Youth Can March, Too 73
18. Want to Help? 77
19. Without a Big Tree . . . Better! 81
20. To Tell or Not to Tell 85
21. Rachel's Joy 89
22. Sea Dad 93
23. Moving—With My Constant Friend 97
24. Estee's Smile 103

25. Trying to Ease the Suffering · · · · · · · · · · · · · · · · · 105
26. Go Ahead—Pray for Anything · · · · · · · · · · · · · · · · 109
27. From the Bible: Listen to Those Older Folks! · · · · · · · · 113
28. Still My Best Friend—For Always · · · · · · · · · · · · · · 117
29. Not Gonna Do It! · 123
30. Carry His Load! · 127
31. More Room—In Nebraska · · · · · · · · · · · · · · · · · · · 131
32. I Can Do All Things through Christ · · · · · · · · · · · · · 135
33. The Quiet One · 141
34. The Baby-Sitter's Club · · · · · · · · · · · · · · · · · · · 147
35. One Bagel—To Go · 153
36. Fellowship's Goal Is Victory off the Field · · · · · · · · · · 157
37. Just Trying to Learn · 161
38. God Will Make a Way · 165

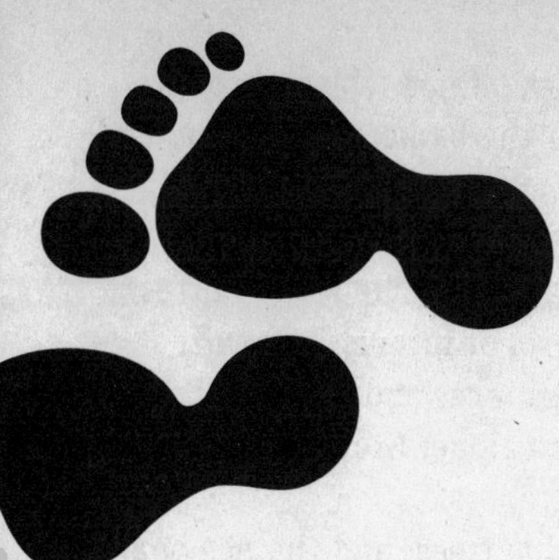

Sudden Storm

FOCUSING IN

"For the first time in a long while I thought about God. . . . Was He real out here in the middle of a blizzard? Could He hear me now—and did He care?"

—Matt, age 14

A thick, gray fog hung over the valley below our log home that damp and dreary Sunday in March, but by midafternoon I needed some fresh air and exercise. So I pulled on my cowboy boots, reached for my down-filled parka, and headed for the back door.

"I'm going to split some wood," I told my dad as I put on my cowboy hat. My words must have alerted Katie, our five-year-old springer spaniel, who seems to understand everything we say. She'd been sound asleep on a rug in front of the fireplace, but now she was at my side, wagging her tail and looking up at me pleadingly.

"Want to come along, girl?" I asked, knowing that was a stupid question. Katie liked a warm fire and often slept on my bed, but she was always ready for an outdoor adventure.

For the next hour, she sat patiently on the hillside, watching me split and stack firewood. "I'm almost done," I told her. "Then we'll go on a quick hike." A few minutes later, I whistled to her, and we were off—across the yard, over the barbed-wire fence, and down the hill to the pasture.

I love exploring the rugged area around our house in the Wildcat Hills of Nebraska's North Platte Valley. The rocky buttes and deep canyons are filled with all sorts of interesting stuff: animal bones, eagles' nests, even rattlesnakes and coyotes. But I've never been afraid of hiking around here alone. Growing up in a place like this makes a kid love the outdoors.

The wind blew through the tall pine trees, and the heavy air felt like it couldn't decide whether to rain or snow. Maybe we'd just go to the shooting range across the pasture and dig up some old shotgun shells. We wouldn't be far from home if the weather turned bad. Katie bounded ahead of me as if she knew right where we were going.

After we got to the range, I was busy digging in the soft dirt when a sudden cold breeze on the back of my neck startled me. Almost immediately I was surrounded by the thickest fog I'd ever seen.

We should get home, I thought.

"Katie!" I called, looking for a familiar landmark. But I couldn't see two feet in front of me. It was like being trapped inside a cloud. "I can find the way home," I kept telling myself as Katie and I walked up a hill. "I can do it."

The wind was blowing more fiercely, and rain began falling in huge, cold drops. I pulled a pair of thin gloves out of my pocket and shoved my hat down on my head.

Finally I reached the barbed-wire fence with relief—and then alarm. This was a three-strand fence. The fence around our property had four strands. There were no three-strand fences in our neighborhood. *We're lost!*

"Help!" I yelled as loudly as I could. Surely someone somewhere would hear me. We had neighbors to the north and west of our house, but the rest of the area was desolate. Was I near home or going in the opposite direction?

"Help!" I cried again. Katie cocked her head and looked at me. The rain started changing to sleet and then to wet flakes of snow.

"Let's go, Katie." I tried not to sound nervous. The sharp wind sliced through my clothes, and my teeth chattered.

I'd forgotten my watch, so I couldn't tell how long we'd been trudging up and down the hills, but the snow looked more like a blizzard now. Big flakes blew in my face. We were coming down a steep hill when suddenly, in front of me, I saw a dark shape—a log fence—and a cabin!

I bounded over the fence and up onto the porch, reached the door, and then stopped. It was padlocked. Peeking in the window, I saw a dusty old magazine on a table. This was someone's summer cabin.

For a moment, I considered breaking in. But that would be vandalism. *Probably the weather will clear soon and we'll find the way home if we just keep going,* I decided. The reasoning seemed logical. Even so, I felt more afraid than I'd ever been in my life.

I turned away from the cabin and set off in the other direction. Several minutes later I came across my own footprints in the snow. Katie and I had been walking in circles!

Just then Katie started sniffing the ground and disappearing in and out of the fog and snow. "Katie!" I yelled, my temper flaring as I ran and tackled her. "Don't leave me. You're all I've got!" She didn't squirm out of my grip. She just looked at me obediently, as if she understood. I buried my face in her soggy brown-and-white coat and cried. "I'm sorry, girl."

I felt totally helpless. For the first time in a long while, I thought about God. I'd always connected God to a Bible or a church, something real that I could see and touch. Was He *real* out here in the middle of a blizzard? Could He hear me now—and did He care?

"God," I prayed, "I'm afraid. Katie and I need You bad. Especially Katie. It's not her fault we're in this mess. Please take care of her."

I knelt there for a couple of minutes, hugging Katie. "I'll bet you're hungry and cold, too," I said, and suddenly remembered I had a cough drop. My fingers were so numb, I had to use my left hand to force my right hand into my jeans to get it. I bit the cough drop in two and gave half to Katie. For a moment, the menthol seemed to warm my mouth. Katie licked her lips.

"Let's go, girl," I said. As darkness descended, I thought of my mom and dad and two brothers at home. Surely they were worried about me by now.

Soon we came to another steep hill. My legs felt like heavy stumps as I climbed it. I sort of skidded down in one motion. At the bottom I slid right into a pool of standing water, hidden by snow and tall grass. For a moment I stood paralyzed as the icy water filled my boots and soaked me up to my knees. Katie jumped in and lapped up the water thirstily. I grabbed her by the collar and lifted her out. She could die if she got soaked and then chilled by the wind. We had to turn around.

As we climbed back up the hill, my legs cramped and my muscles felt as if they were tearing off the bones. The snow swirled into drifts around me. I felt heavy and weak. All I wanted to do was lie down and go to sleep. I spotted a pine tree with big, protective branches and crawled underneath. Katie laid her head on my chest. But after a while she started whining, nudging me in the face with her cold, wet nose. She wanted us to go on.

I felt kind of delirious, but said, "Okay, we'll try to keep going." Every step was an effort. Again I found a tree and crawled underneath, but now my whole body shivered so uncontrollably that I banged around on the cold, hard ground like a wooden puppet. Parts of me felt so strangely numb that I hardly cared.

Katie crawled in beside me. She was shivering, too, so I unzipped my down-filled parka, which was so wet that it stretched wildly out of shape, and I zipped us both into it. We must have warmed each other up, because soon Katie squirmed out of the parka and lay down at my feet. I looked up through the branches of the tree, thinking it must be nearly morning. "Please, God,"

I prayed, "no matter what happens to me, please protect Katie. I don't want her to die."

I couldn't see God or hear Him, but I knew He was watching over us. I heard some coyotes off in the distance, but I wasn't afraid. I fell asleep.

I don't remember much else except struggling back to consciousness and seeing some daylight. Where was Katie? I looked in horror at a pile of snow under my feet. Was she frozen under there?

"Katie!" I shouted. Suddenly I heard a rustling sound on the hillside as she crawled back under the tree and licked my face. "Good girl," I said, still feeling only half-conscious. Then I heard the sound of an airplane. I knew I had to get out into the open.

I concentrated to make my muscles work and slowly rolled out from under the tree. It had stopped snowing.

I tried to stand up but couldn't, so I crawled toward an open field. I don't know how long it took. I finally collapsed in the snow.

The next thing I heard was a muffled voice calling my name. I tried to respond.

"Katie . . . ," I mumbled. "Is Katie okay?"

"Katie's fine. She's home, resting by the fireplace." The voice was my mother's. I was in a hospital bed. She and my father were telling me that rescuers in an airplane had spotted me a couple of miles from home about one o'clock that afternoon, facedown and motionless, with Katie by my side. My body temperature had dropped dangerously low in the night, when the windchill got below zero. They told me I was now in intensive care, being treated for frostbite and hypothermia.

"The doctor says it's a miracle that you survived," my mother said.

For the next few days in the hospital and then back home again sitting by the fire recovering with Katie, I thought a lot about the doctor's words. I don't know whether or not it was a miracle that I survived. What I do know is that I had another friend besides Katie out there, and I never would have made it without Him. He's a friend who became real to me that night. A friend I'll keep for life.

—Matt Meyers

Young Believer Connection

Check out the character study of Elijah on page 471 of the *Young Believer Bible.* This man had to travel the wilderness often, but God took care of him—even dropping food by "raven post"!

READ: 1 Kings 17:1-7

Think about It!

In what areas of life do you need God's protection and help? Have you prayed about this?

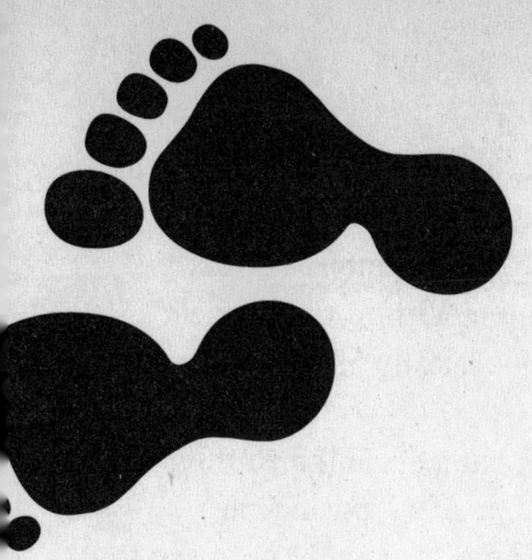

2 Out of Control

FOCUSING IN

"My life is my own; I am in control—or not."

—Mike, age 18

Snow flew high as the sharp, metallic edge of my board cut deep into the fresh powder of the virgin slope. Leaning into the turn, I sucked in the cold fresh air of the European Alps. The crystallized snow sparkled and danced as it reflected the setting sun. Only the swish of my board and the low whistle of the wind could be heard.

I'd been waiting all year for spring break. The snow was deep, the slopes fresh, and the usual crowd of annoying skiers . . . nonexistent! I was free, and I was invincible. I had been on a board for over five years, during which I'd developed my skills—and far too much confidence in my abilities.

During those few years my attitude had become, "My life is my own; I am in control." I took every opportunity to push the limits as far as possible. However, today I was to discover just how far those limits could be pushed.

Usually about half a day into a week of snowboarding, I find that the regular slopes become monotonous, and—as any decent snowboarder would—I begin searching for variants. The first couple of days were quite typical: steep mountain trails, sheer cliffs, light sprains, monstrous jumps—basically all the action you could take.

Then it happened: after stretching and straining to the maximum capacity, I pushed the limit too far. After exiting the gondola, I made up my mind to hike the rest of the way to the top of the mountain and carve some fresh powder before I met up with the main slope again. It was simple enough: if you don't like their trails, make your own.

So there I was, slicing up the new powder, reveling in self-confidence. I could see the slope, about eighty feet below me to my left. I eased the nose of my board down and began to plummet toward the slope, mentally planning the rest of my descent. Suddenly, the edge of my slope came into view, a sheer drop-off where it met the main slope. I knew I couldn't jump it since it would be a big drop before I slammed onto the totally flat, compacted snow of the main slope.

Instinct kicked in. I leaned and took a sharp right turn back up the hill. Tension released as I completed the turn a good three feet from the edge. But then my stomach lurched as that solid three feet of snow dropped away from beneath me, avalanching over the edge.

I was thrust into thin air. Who could guess what lay below me? I wondered what my dog was doing right then. Probably curled up in front of a warm fire in the dining room. With a rush, time resumed, and my chest slammed into the edge of the drop-off.

Desperately, I clawed at the edge, but my well-padded gloves hadn't been designed for cliff-hanging. Methodically I shoved the sharp edge of my board into the side of the cliff, knowing that—if it could catch—it would hold me suspended. But I was already moving too fast, and as my board glanced off the face I lost all balance and plunged backward in a reverse dive.

And then—darkness. I couldn't see a thing, I couldn't breathe. I also couldn't be dead; this was way too cold to be heaven. I tried to move but couldn't. Slowly my thoughts began to gather, and I remembered hitting the snow headfirst and catching a glimpse of the avalanche that had buried me instantly. It then occurred to me to move my legs, which caused my board to move. That was strange. Usually when a boarder slams, it's the board that gets stuck.

My head was also starting to ache from all the blood rushing to it. *Hey—I'm upside down!* My head, chest, and legs were buried deep beneath the snow, while my feet and snowboard stuck out. Thinking back, I realize the sight must have been quite comical, if not downright hilarious. But right then my mouth was too full of snow to laugh.

As I tried to dig the snow out from under my back to obtain a sitting position, I began to wonder why I felt no significant pain. I had fallen headfirst toward the hard-packed slope; I should be dead, or at least seriously injured. Then I recalled how the snow had given way beneath me and realized I had sent down a dump-truckload of the soft stuff, which accounted for the unusually gentle landing. Had I not landed directly on that soft snow, I'd have been a goner.

Silently, I praised God for sparing my life and then popped my head out of the snow to take in my surroundings. For the second time that day reality walked up and slapped me in the face. On either side of where I sat, still half buried in snow, two large boulders jutted through the whiteness all around me.

At that moment, I realized just how much control over my life I really had—none. By all logical standards I should be dead, or in a wheelchair for the rest of my life. For the first time in my life I began to see and accept God's sovereign hand on my life.

He is the one in control, whether I'm on my board—or sitting safe and dry by the fire, nursing a few monster bruises.

—Mike Walt

YB Young Believer

Young Believer Connection

Check out the character study of the apostle Paul on page 1437 of the *Young Believer Bible.* He survived a real catastrophe—a shipwreck and a poisonous snakebite!

READ: Acts 27:27–28:6

Think about It!

Recall the worst danger you've ever experienced. How was God there with you, protecting you? What did you learn?

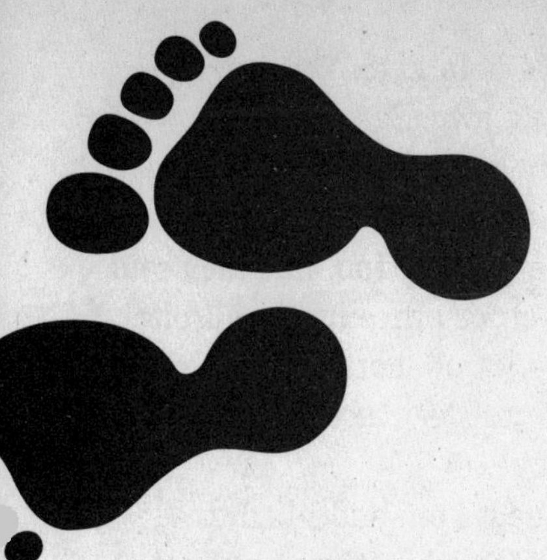

Needing Help—But What Kind?

FOCUSING IN

"It's amazing what kids will tell you if you make the first move."

—Kurt, age 15

I know, Christians are supposed to encourage one another. But how exactly are you supposed to do that? Look, I'm only a fifteen-year-old guy, but I've spent a lot of time trying to scope this out. I mean, you want to help somebody, but how do you figure out what that person needs? You'll understand what I mean when you hear my story.

I was six years old at the time, and here's what I was thinking. . . .

My big brother, Kyle, has this thing called "lookeemya" or something. It hurts him a lot. It's like his bones are falling apart, and his hair comes out from the medicine he gets. I feel sorry for him. I hear Mom and Dad crying for him at night. They think I'm asleep, but sometimes I start crying too.

One day Mom and Dad said I could help Kyle. They said I didn't have to. But I could decide on my own. See, my bones were good, and I could give Kyle some of my bones (like the inside part that makes blood), but only if I wanted to share.

At first I thought I would have to get sick too. But they said it would just hurt a little bit at the doctor's office in the hospital. So I said okay. And then I had to get a lot of shots—which really, *really* hurt. And then they made me go to sleep at the hospital, so I can't tell you what happened after that.

When I woke up, I had some bandages on, and I had to eat yucky food at the hospital for a whole day while they gave me some more blood. But everybody else was happy. They said it was a success, and Kyle would be better for a long time.

Okay, so I went back home. About a month later, Kyle came home too. He gave me this big hug. He still looked sick to me, without his hair and everything. But he smiled at me a lot.

He said he would take me to the park to look for frogs. And yesterday he did.

That was me way back then.

I think back, and I realize it was pretty easy to help Kyle because everybody told me it would be a good thing to do. They said how much it would help and everything. But nothing like that has ever happened again. I mean, nobody has walked up to me and said, "Hey, Kurt, here's exactly what you can do to make somebody's life a lot better."

So now I'm thinking it's mostly up to me to find out that kind of information on my own. I have to stay alert and look for opportunities to help people. Not like it's a big pain or anything. Actually, it's kind of fun. All I do is sit back and observe the people around me. For instance, maybe I'll be at a party where I'll see some kid who looks like he could be having more fun. If I really watch, I might see something in his eyes that says he's just faking his smile or laughter. Maybe later I'll talk to him and say something like, "You know, I'm stressed out right now with school and work." (I don't make these things up, of course. If I'm stressed, I just say it.) That usually frees up the other person to talk about what's going on in his life.

It's amazing what kids will tell you if you make the first move like that—if you show you're ready to listen and care about them. I've had guys and girls tell me their problems, and I've always kept their secrets. And lots of times I've figured out how to help. But usually just being there for them is enough.

And believe me, this isn't something that can just happen between teens. Take what happened at my church, as an example. I met a lady there who has a rare bone disease. The pastor said we should pray for her because she was going in for a "marrow aspiration" (that's when they stick needles into your pelvic bones—about fifty times!—to remove blood from the inside). Anyway, I did my sit-back-and-observe thing for a while, and I could tell this lady was pretty scared about the whole thing. And she's not young, either. I mean, she is up there in age, like seventy or something. But you know she's human too, just like me.

So I went over to her after the church service, but at first I didn't know exactly what to say. So I smiled, and I even put my arm around her shoulders. (Can you believe that? Hey, I was just following my instincts at this point.) I said to her, "Mrs. Chetwood, I remember giving my bone marrow to my brother, and I want to let you know that everything turned out okay."

Now that wasn't much, I know. I don't even remember what she said back to me. But I remember there were tears in her eyes.

I really think I helped her.

I know it made me feel good.

—Kurt's story, as told by Ruth Reed

Young Believer Connection

Check out the character study of Joshua on page 280 of the *Young Believer Bible.* Joshua must have wondered how best to encourage his people as they faced battles with those already living in the Promised Land.

READ: Joshua 4:1-24

Think about It!

When was the last time you had an opportunity to encourage someone? What kind of response did you receive?

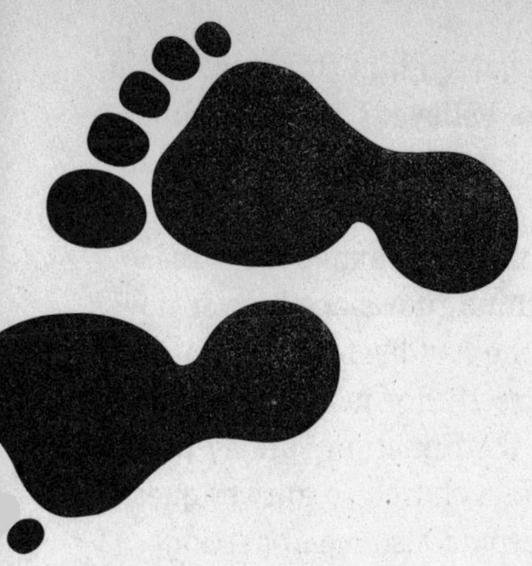

4 The Chase

FOCUSING IN

"I just want to believe for myself."

—Walker, age 14

Walker took off running through the woods, his pursuers close behind him. They were dressed in camouflage and yelled into walkie-talkies. He could hear one of them breathing hard behind him, trying to catch up. Walker picked up speed as he cut through some shrubs. The thick branches scratched his arms and legs as he ran, but he didn't stop. After a few minutes he dropped down beside a fallen log, his heart pounding. He listened for any sign of pursuit.

Silence. He had lost them.

Where are my friends? He and Travis had stuck together at first. They had left the lodge just behind the first group of campers to escape. But then the guards came running around the corner after them, and everyone split up. *I hope no one got caught,* he thought, rising to his knees.

Just that afternoon their pastor had taught them all about Christian history. Walker had been surprised to learn that the first Christians were persecuted for their faith. Many of them died because they believed in Jesus. It had gotten him thinking. Could he stand up for Jesus when no one else believed? The next thing on the schedule had been swimming, so he forgot all about what the pastor said.

It had been four days since confirmation camp began. His parents had dragged him there, explaining that since he was now thirteen, he could "confirm" the faith he had been taught since birth. He could believe in Jesus for himself, not just because his parents did. For most of the students, Confirmation Sunday would involve standing up in front of the whole church to answer questions about their faith. For Walker, it would also mean getting baptized. But first, all the students went to camp.

There had been a family dinner the first night of camp, with a bunch of songs and a skit afterwards. Walker had grabbed his parents before they left and begged, "Can I go with you? I don't even know if I want to get baptized."

"Give the camp a try, Walker," his mom had said. "If you are still miserable by Wednesday morning, give me a call."

But he hadn't needed to call. During the day the campers swam, played games, and attended Bible classes, which weren't as boring as he had expected. Each evening they did something fun, like capture the flag or sailing lessons. Then they went to worship service, complete with songs and skits. Walker had burst out laughing at the skit on Monday and decided he liked hearing his leader play the guitar—so worship wasn't all that bad, either. In fact, Walker was having a blast.

But now here he was, tearing through the woods like a hunted rabbit. He began to wonder all over again. His pastor had said that there were Christians in places like China and Sudan that were still persecuted for their faith. They were being hunted in the woods just like this, all because they took a stand for Jesus. *It must take a lot of courage. This is only a game, but it's real for those Christians.*

He ran behind a tree and paused to catch his breath. *Could I do that?* he wondered. *Could I take a stand for Jesus?* The woods were quiet. His breathing sounded loud. So did his heartbeat—he could hear the blood pumping hard in his ears. But in that eerie silence, something happened. For the first time, Walker knew that he wanted to believe in Jesus. He wanted to follow Jesus for the rest of his life. Not because his parents did. Not because his friends did. But because Jesus was calling him, personally, to do it.

He began to pray: *Jesus, I know there are people dying every day because they choose to follow you. Give me the courage to stand up for you like that—to be willing to go against the flow. Even when everything seems hopeless, Lord, and I'm the only one, I will believe in you.*

He took a deep breath and plunged into the woods. His footsteps in the leaves made a lot of noise. The crunching was so loud that he didn't hear the guard coming up behind him until it was too late.

"Gotchya!" the guy said, grabbing Walker by the shirt. Walker flopped on the forest floor in surrender as two more guards in camouflage approached.

"You take him to jail," his attacker said to one of them, "and we'll round up the others." His attacker ran off, followed by one of the guards.

"Hi, Ashley," Walker said.

Ashley had green and black paint smeared all over her face, and leaves stuck in her hair.

"Did you do this at camp last year, too?"

She nodded. "Katie and I got caught right away, and then Scott helped us escape from jail. We ran in the woods forever until we found the meeting spot where everyone was waiting. We had to promise to keep the game a secret, so it wouldn't spoil the surprise for next year's class."

"Well, your class sure kept the secret. We had no idea what

was coming. We got together for worship like we usually do, and then all of sudden these people in camouflage were banging on the door."

Ashley laughed. "I can still remember how scared I was when the guards crashed through the doors and told us we were all under house arrest. But then I saw that one of the guards was Adam, and I knew it was just a game."

Everyone sitting around the circle looked scared to death. But they were also laughing in a shaky sort of way—as if they had just been to a haunted house at Halloween. As Walker joined them, they all began talking at once, telling stories about their captures and escapes.

Finally, their leader arrived. "How did it feel to be persecuted for your faith?" she asked.

They discussed how scared they were at first, and how tough it was to stand up for their faith—even when they knew it was all a game. But Walker didn't speak. He wasn't ready to tell anyone yet about the decision he had made on the run in the woods.

The camp leader made them promise to keep the game a secret for the next year, and the kids all sneaked back through the woods to the lodge. A few days later, while Walker and his mom were folding his camp laundry, he decided to open up about his experience.

"Mom," he said, "I want to be baptized."

She stopped folding his socks and stared. "Really?"

"Really."

"You're not just saying that to please Dad and me?"

"No. I really want to be baptized."

"Well, wonderful! But what changed your mind?"

He paused, folding the pair of shorts he had worn that night in the woods. They were still stained and had little rips everywhere. Pulling at one of the rips thoughtfully, he shrugged. "I just want to believe for myself."

His mother came around the table and gave him a hug. "That takes a lot of courage. I'm proud of you."

The very next Confirmation Sunday, Walker made his decision public and was baptized. There, in front of the whole church, he took his stand for Jesus, just as the early Christians did so many years ago.

—Walker's story, as told by Sarah Arthur

Young Believer Connection

YB Young Believer

Check out the character study of Daniel on page 1098 of the *Young Believer Bible*. This young man had to decide whether to keep praying or quit praying—just because the government told him to stop worshiping the Lord.

READ: Daniel 6:1-28

Think about It!

Think: Do I basically have my parents' faith or my own faith? On a scale of 1 to 8 below, decide where you are right now:

1 2 3 4 5 6 7 8

Whatever Mom and Dad believe—that's me!	Trying to stand up on my own "faith legs"	Don't care who knows it—I stand for Jesus.

What could you do this week to help you move one step closer to a number *8*—a faith that is fully your own?

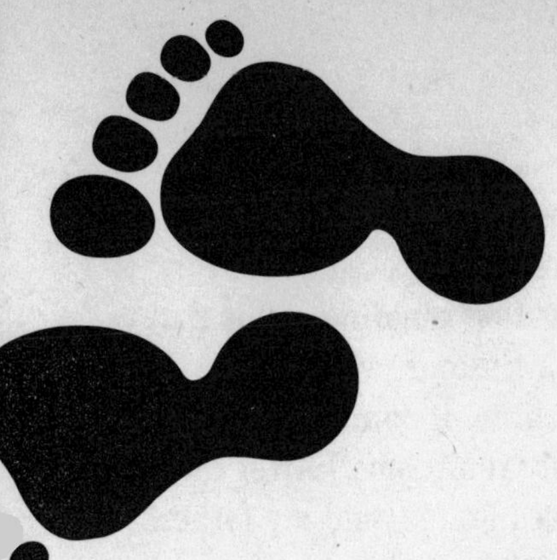

Love, Hate, and Tears

FOCUSING IN

"My whole world has been turned upside down!"

—Tim, age 11

I walked up to the pulpit in front of the whole church to share my heart about what it meant to me that my family, all of us together, were going to live on a poor Caribbean island. I knew beforehand that I was going to speak, and I was deathly afraid. My feelings were churning inside. I was leaving school, grandparents, buddies on the block—all those familiar surroundings that made saying good-bye seem impossible. It was starting to hit me—losing my comfortable "American kid" life—no more bike rides to the park, no more sledding down snow-packed sidewalks, no more TV cartoons.

Worst of all . . . no more junk food.

Anyway, I felt the pressure to say the right things. "This is awe-inspiring, and I really feel God's peace tonight" or "I'd rather help the poor than anything else."

But as I opened my mouth, I was still wondering what would tumble out. . . .

You see, when my parents founded the new missionary agency—New Missions—we lived in tents on the Haitian oceanfront for three months while we constructed our first building. (This first structure, made of cement block with a tin roof, would serve as our housing, office, kitchen, and medical clinic. It sounds big, but it was a small U-shaped building with only ten rooms.) After that initial stage, we came back to the United States, and my father continued traveling back and forth from Massachusetts, where he works as a pastor, to Haiti. So, once my three months of living in a tent were over and we moved into the building, I could think back to "camping" on the beach and say, "Cool!" Then, after we started the mission, we could come back to America during the summer to preach in churches and raise money for the mission.

Before the year was out, though, we decided to move to Haiti full-time. That was the moment in my life when everything radically changed. That was the test of sacrifice. It was the test of love and the test of how much I'd give for God. It was all coming to a head for me as I was just hitting my teenage years.

So then we had a "sending service" at church. It was a time for the people to gather and send us off with their blessing and a plea for God's blessing, too. After all, we were crossing into another culture.

The church was packed. We had all the good old missionary songs, the slides, and Dad's preaching. Then he asked me to come and tell everyone what it meant for me to make this monumental commitment to Haiti.

What could I say? Suddenly the preacher's kid would be a missionary kid. I'd be a role model of servanthood, committed to doing good, giving my best, no matter the cost. (Oh, and also, my whole world has been turned upside down. Which is just a side issue, right? Well, no, not to me.)

I opened my mouth and . . . cried.

I ran off that stage as fast as I could. There was an attic leading to the rooftop of the church, and that's where I headed. I whimpered my way up a steep ladder in a dark, dreary hallway, opened the door, and got swallowed up in darkness. I knew no one would find me; no one would see me as I listened for the sounds of church to die down.

What drove me to that point of speechlessness? It wasn't just one thing—it was everything. It was seeing my parents so willing to sacrifice, so ready to give up a beautiful church, a nice clean Victorian home, a gleaming white sailboat, for love of a few half-starved strangers. Yet I was watching my own life crumbling into that same pool of sacrifice. Choosing with all my heart to do it, and choosing *not* to do it, too. . . .

I compared what my parents were giving up with what I was giving up, and I felt ashamed. I hated feeling the shame. I wanted to hold on to my faith while stuffing down an unformed rage. But I was suppressing a love, too, that wanted to encircle the whole world.

What do you do when love and hate come together? I know for sure that it makes you speechless. I just can't begin to name all the blessings, all the pain, all the extremes of God's plans for me.

Have you been there, too?

—Tim DeTellis

Young Believer Connection

Check out the I Believe statement "God chose people to share his message" on page 948 of the *Young Believer Bible.* Remember that reaching out to all peoples is God's plan for us.

READ: Isaiah 61:1-2

Think about It!

How far away is your personal mission field? Could it be next door? at school? or across the ocean?

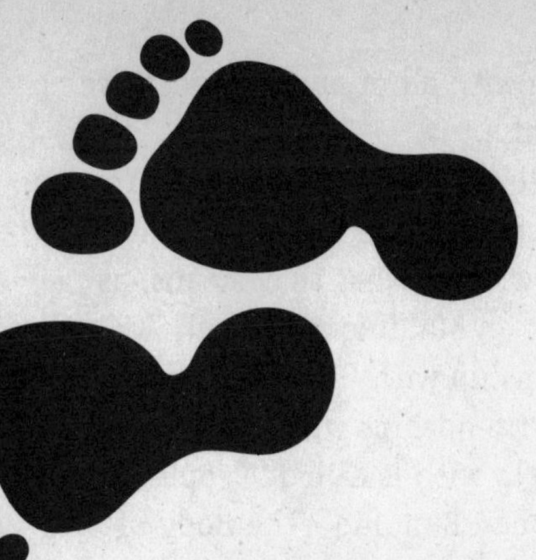

Toughest Job You'll Ever Love

FOCUSING IN

"With all the 'things' we have in our country, lots of people, including me, become distracted from God. That's why we go to Mexico."

—John, age 18

We've been driving now for twenty-four hours straight, and I'm ready for my last American meal. I pull the bus into the parking lot of a diner near the city limits of Odessa, Texas, and turn off the engine. Suddenly everybody inside the bus springs to life and pushes for the door. I can't blame them, really. Little do these rookies realize what they're getting into on this trip. For nearly everyone aboard, this will be an experience they'll always remember.

Don Camberlin, a great man who once took this journey with us, said, "We start with changing a house, a block, a town, a city, a country, a world." And that's just how I feel. I want to change the world—one house at a time.

I've helped lead this trip for the past four or five years, but I've been going since I was in the fourth grade. Usually at least eighty people and I go for the purpose of building churches,

Sunday schools, and houses. But even with all of our resources, we cannot solve everyone's need for a house.

Little do we realize this is a small part of the experience. Yes, we do build houses, but even more than that, we build horizontal and vertical relationships. You might wonder what that means, as I once did. As an individual, you work on building a vertical (up-and-down, top-to-bottom) relationship with God and numerous, lifelong horizontal (side-to-side) friendships with people your age and with others. The ministry I help with is called "People Building People" with the motto of "Body Building—the Body of Christ." A very appropriate name for what we do.

I finish my burger and check my watch. We have just one hour until we hop back into the packed fifteen-passenger vans. Where are we going? you might ask. My fellow travelers and I are heading out for ten days in Juárez, Mexico.

Many kids feel that this trip requires leaving your home, but I think of the place as a second home for me. That's why I'm going to stay for two months. Actually, I feel safer in Mexico than I do in my own town back East because of the love of the Mexicans and their trust in Jesus Christ. I have never seen people who depend so completely on God. I can say that I have never met someone from the United States who has committed everything to God in the way that many Mexican families have done. In fact, I once heard that in Juarez "98 percent of the people own 2 percent of the wealth, and 2 percent of the people have 98 percent of the wealth." That is quite a staggering difference among the people.

Have you ever seen poor people in America? Many have nothing except for the clothes on their backs. "Why don't we help our own?" some may ask. Well, our government in America has many different programs to help them. In Mexico, the government doesn't help as much with the poverty in their country. Americans have many ways to overcome poverty, but Mexican families must depend upon God alone to provide.

So, since the end of my sophomore year in high school I have been leading the construction of houses for our Christian brothers and sisters in Mexico. I've been honored to lead the construction of three single houses, 22 feet by 11 feet, and two double-wide houses, 30 feet by 15 feet. We build from nothing but sand, and when we are done there is a sturdy house. The house has a roof, stucco on the outside, drywall, electrical wiring, doors, and windows. (By the way, this all happens in less than three and a half days!) A house like that is a mansion compared to the smelly old cardboard shacks. (It is extremely hard to explain what they live in, but I guarantee that you have never seen happier people than when they move out of a shack!)

Here's the thing that really gets me: I thought I would see Mexicans crying and being sad all the time. Well, I do see some cry . . . but out of *joy* when they receive the keys to their brand-new houses! They are all so grateful to us for allowing the Lord to use us to help them. So, you see, this trip is not only about building houses but also about building relationships.

Also, this trip is unique in the fact that there are no distractions in this part of Mexico: no television, Internet, or video games. Instead, many of us spend time thinking about people and God, and this makes it easier for us to feel God's presence with us. With all the "things" we have in our country, lots of people, including me, become distracted from God. That's why we go to Mexico.

Now that I've finished my freshman year at the University of Cincinnati, I'm able to live in Mexico for the summer. I asked myself, *Would I rather be making money or doing something for the Lord?*

It was an obvious choice for me and my friend Dan Pawlak. With People Building People, we've constructed over twenty-two homes, churches, and Sunday schools.

Until now, two trips are the most we've done in one summer.

Because of God's great timing, Dan will join me in leading six trips to Mexico this summer. I figure the two of us will be able to impact many more people for the Lord.

With God's unending guidance, we plan to lead people from all over the nation—and the world—to experience God's love and provision in a very big way. But first, we've got to get everyone back on the bus. As somebody once said, "The longest journey begins with the first step." For me, a great house begins with that first nail.

—John Gadsby

YB Young Believer

Young Believer Connection

Check out the character study of Priscilla and Aquila on page 1484 of the *Young Believer Bible.* They had the opportunity to travel with the apostle Paul and tell others about God.

READ: Acts 18; Romans 16:3; 1 Corinthians 16:19

Think about It!

If you were to let go of some of your entertainments and other distractions, could you focus on what Jesus is calling you to do? Are there any people close to you who need help? How about people far away from you?

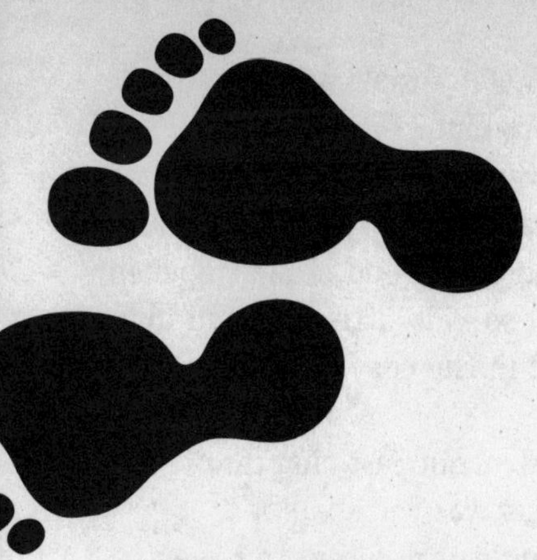

7 Keeping the Faith in Hard Times

FOCUSING IN

"Sometimes we get so caught up in winning and losing that it's hard for a lot of guys."

—Demoine, age 22

The Nebraska football player wanted to cry. He wanted to curse Coach Frank Solich. He wanted to quit the team.

"I kept thinking, 'What did I do wrong?' " said senior rush end Demoine Adams, called to Solich's office the Monday morning after the Huskers' blowout loss to Iowa State in September and told he would no longer start. "I was so hurt," he said, speaking to a group of Lincoln East athletes. "I had been a three-year Blackshirt. I had an awesome season last year. Nothing was going to stop me. This was going to be my blowout year."

Instead, it was a blow to his pride.

Adams didn't say what he felt that day—that he was angry and hurt. He stayed quiet. In his head he heard a Bible verse: Be quick to listen, slow to speak, slow to become angry (James 1:19, NIV).

Before being called to Solich's office, Adams had been lifting weights. After, he didn't want go back to the weight room. He didn't want to go to class. He drove to The Mill, a coffeehouse downtown, where he sat for hours alone at a table and stared out the window. Drinking nothing. Just thinking. *There's no way I'm going to practice today,* he thought. *Everyone will be looking at me, knowing, feeling sorry.* "It was like I had no strength," Adams said.

Yet again in his life, Adams called out to God. Adams opened with a prayer. He blessed the dozen or so kids sitting around him, curled up on couches and cross-legged in the cozy basement of Mark and Angie Klasek's home.

The Klaseks are "coaches" of the Lincoln East chapter of Fellowship of Christian Athletes. Sunday was the chapter's bimonthly "huddle," and the kids thought it was cool to have a Husker in the huddle.

Adams opened his Bible. "I want to share with you my favorite Bible verse: 'I can do all things through Christ, who gives me strength'" [Philippians 4:13, paraphrased].

Then Adams gave his testimony, telling how a short, fat kid from Pine Bluff, Arkansas, who thought he was stupid, grew to live for God. "Kids used to laugh at me because I stuttered," he said. So to be cool, he skipped school. He didn't do his homework. He hung out with kids who drank and did drugs. "Even though I looked cool to everyone else, I still felt empty," he said. "I knew it wasn't me."

When Adams was in junior high, his father got saved and started teaching him about God. Adams began to pray. God gave him strength. First, God separated him from the "junk" in his life. The bad friends. The bad TV. The bad music. The bad thoughts that he wasn't good enough to play college ball. Or even go to college. Then God saturated him with the desire to study the Bible and preach to his friends . . . by example.

Now Adams, 22, preaches from the pulpit. He is a full-time preacher while studying for his master's in counseling psychology and while preparing for his final game as a Husker: the Independence Bowl in Shreveport. This football season, he said, God has tested him through adversity.

Losing his starting job was difficult. But it tested his faith. And his faith came out stronger. It was a lesson in pride. And it was a lesson many Husker teammates have learned this season, too, Adams continued.

More Huskers have started showing up at the Bible studies that Adams leads along with fellow Husker Aaron Terpening. More Huskers have started showing up at FCA meetings. And more Huskers have started showing up at church. After the Huskers' loss to Oklahoma State in October, about 20 Huskers came to the Angelic Temple Church in Lincoln to hear Adams preach.

"Since we started losing, it's like everybody's down and they're looking for answers," Adams said. "They're looking for Jesus Christ. He is showing them the right perspective. Sometimes we get so caught up in winning and losing that it's hard for a lot of guys."

—Demoine's story, as told by Colleen Kenney

YB Young Believer

Young Believer Connection

Check out David's directions to his son Solomon on page 571 of the *Young Believer Bible.* He wanted to lead his nation in building God's temple. But God said no. David had to wait on the sidelines until his son Solomon would build the temple instead.

READ: 1 Chronicles 28

Think about It!

Have you ever been "put on the sidelines" when you really wanted to be involved? How did you handle it? What kinds of prayers did you say?

Originally published as "Huskers' Adams Keeps Faith in Hard Times," by Colleen Kenney, in the *Lincoln Journal Star,* Lincoln, Nebraska, 23 December 2002 (Monday, BC cycle. Section: Sports News). Used with permission.

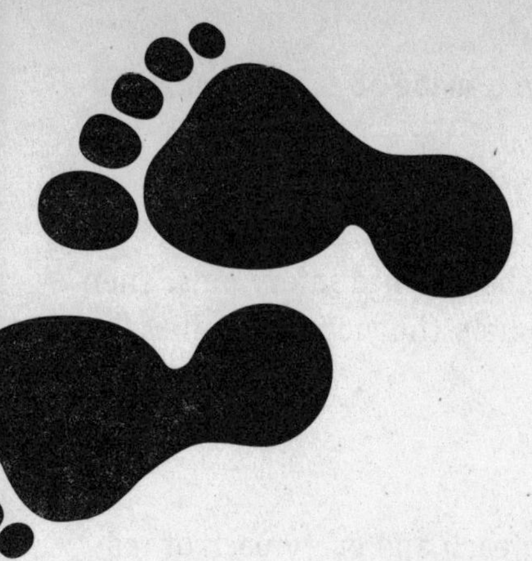

Safety Pins and Postmen

FOCUSING IN

"I want to know what my hands can do to help!"

—Joel, age 10

"What can I do to help?" my son Joel asked. The shocking news of September 11, 2001, spread fast, even to ears thought too young to comprehend. But Joel did understand. He knew his nation was wounded and that many lives had been changed forever. He understood that people needed each other in a way he'd never seen before.

"But, really, Mom, what can I do? What can I do to help the families, the kids, and grown-ups?"

"Joel, you can pray. You know, praying is probably the most powerful thing you can do."

"Mom, I've already prayed, and more than one time a day! I want to know what my *hands* can do to help!"

I was now thinking on overload. I had no idea what a ten-year-old could do to help this situation, much less use his hands to do it. I added to my prayer list "an idea for Joel so he can help victims of September 11."

A day later, the thought came. "Joel, I've got it! Do you

remember the beaded cross pin that you made at camp a couple of summers ago?"

"The one that was made of safety pins?"

"Yes! Why can't you try to design an American flag? You know—stringing red, white, and blue beads onto safety pins. Then maybe you could collect donations to help the victims' families."

Off to the craft store we went, buying each and every pack of red, white, and blue beads that we could find. As if on a scavenger hunt, we shopped for and bought safety pins. Seventeen thousand safety pins, to be exact! Joel named his project "Helping Hands" and even found some friends who were willing to help assemble the flag pins. Joel then made signs that boldly read, "My Gift to You When You Donate to the Red Cross." Within weeks, Joel had managed to collect five thousand dollars in donations.

After such an overwhelming task, Joel's hands were tired. His fingers were tender. They had not yet recovered from "accidental pokes" from the sharp points of the safety pins when he heard the horrific news—a postal worker had died from anthrax.

Again, the questions came flying. "Mom, what is anthrax? How did it get there? Aren't the post-office workers scared?"

I answered each question to the best of my knowledge, but then came a question that I had no answer to: "Mom, what's the name of our postman?" A lump formed in my throat as I realized that we had lived in our home for ten years, and I had no idea of the name of the person delivering our mail each day.

"Do you think our postman is scared?" Joel asked.

The next afternoon he stood next to our mailbox, singing to pass the time, until he saw the wheels of the mail truck approaching. With a smile, Joel introduced himself to the mail carrier. "Hi, I'm Joel. I live here."

"Glad to meet you, Joel. My name's Jimmy."

"Are ya scared?"

"Scared?"

"Yeah, about the anthrax."

"We're doing our jobs, and we're being extra careful. Thanks for asking," Jimmy said just before he drove away.

I heard the front door of our house shut with gusto. "Mom!" Joel shouted. "His name is Jimmy! Our mailman's name is Jimmy!"

Within seconds, Joel met me in the kitchen. "I want to do more. Mom, I want to do something for Jimmy. How many friends at the post office do you think Jimmy has?"

"Maybe twenty?" I guessed as I got on the phone and called the post office. Two hundred and five was the count the postal worker gave. Evidently, Jimmy was both well known and well liked at the post office.

Again, Joel and I went to the craft stores and bought every red, white, and blue bead we found. Due to their shortage of safety pins, we made calls, buying pins directly from the manufacturer. Joel posted his sign, and Helping Hands was back in business.

This time it was different. Joel wasn't collecting donations. He was creating gifts of encouragement—a flag pin for every postal worker in the city of Orange, California. After completing his task, Joel typed a note and printed it out, 205 times:

> *I have made you this flag pin to remind you that people in our city appreciate the work you do for us. I am praying for you as you deliver our mail. I know that GOD WILL BLESS AMERICA!*
>
> *Love, Joel*

While Joel was attaching the notes to the flag pins, Allison, a neighbor friend, stopped by. "Hey, can I help?" she asked.

"Yeah. You've come just in time. I want to get these in the mailbox before the mailman comes."

Joel quickly grabbed a pen, and Allison added her name to the notes. Sitting side by side, they worked until each flag pin was accompanied by a note. They then boxed up the couple hundred flag pins, tied a bow around them, and added a card that read "To: Jimmy and Friends." They placed the package in our mailbox and raised the red flag.

With a task well done, Joel and Allison went off to play. It wasn't until later that afternoon that I got the call.

"Hi, are you Joel's mom?" the voice asked.

"Yes."

"Well, you must be very proud of your son. I am the postmaster in Orange, and I'd like to know if you would bring Joel and Allison to the post office tomorrow morning about 9:00. I thought it would be great if they themselves could pass out the flag pins to the mail carriers."

The next morning we went to the post office, where the postmaster had divided the 205 postal workers into three groups. Three times Joel and Allison took front stage, encouraging the mail carriers and handing out pins. Tears gathered in some of the postal workers' eyes as they accepted their pins from Joel and Allison. "I think it's fantastic that you two took the time to do this and to come and talk to us," one man said while shaking Joel's hand. Others offered hugs and words of thanks. Before the morning was over, Joel and Allison were made honorary mail carriers of Orange, California.

—Joel's story, as told by Janet Lynn Mitchell

YB Young Believer

Young Believer Connection

Check out the character study of Barnabas on page 1393 of the *Young Believer Bible*. This Bible character's name means "son of encouragement." He knew how important it was to encourage others in their work.

READ: Acts 11:19-26

Think about It!

When I'm working on a project with others, I'm usually . . .

¤ organizing and helping things go smoothly
¤ complaining about how tired I am
¤ watching to make sure others don't do less work than me
¤ helping when somebody is having trouble
¤ criticizing people for their mistakes
¤ complimenting people on their good job

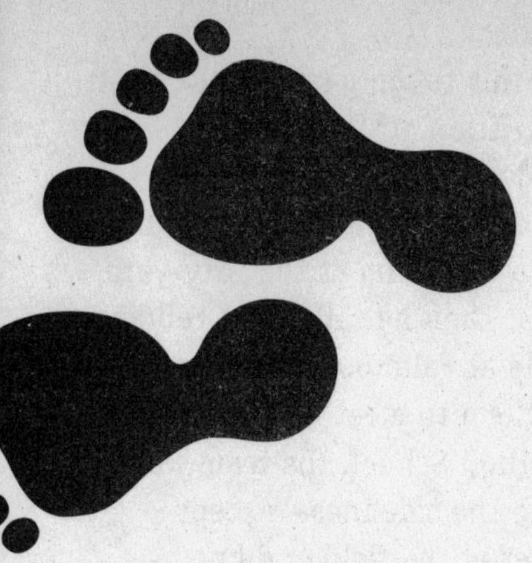

9 Brock's Prayer

FOCUSING IN

"First, I want to thank my Lord and Savior, Jesus Christ. He died for me; I want to live for Him."

—Brock, age 16

Game over. Yes, game definitely over. I played my heart out, Lord. And we lost! Now it's time to walk back on the field and keep my word.

Slowly Brock Farrel walked from the bench where his teammates were grabbing helmets and equipment. Brock would join them for the solemn bus ride home, but first he had an appointment to keep at the fifty-yard line.

Brock quietly knelt in his dirty uniform, his helmet on the ground. He didn't know exactly what to expect from his teammates, especially since they had lost the game to Fallbrook. He waited, eyes closed, offering a silent prayer of gratitude in front of his classmates and the happy Fallbrook fans in the stands.

Dripping with sweat after losing this tough game, Brock knelt in order to show solidarity with all Christian athletes. When he was a junior, in his first game as a starting varsity quarterback, he wanted to make a more public statement of his faith. He called all his football buddies and asked them to meet him at the fifty-yard line to kneel and pray after the games. Then he called the Fellowship of Christian Athletes (FCA) huddle at Fallbrook, the team they were competing against, and invited them to meet him there too.

It was a bad loss for San Marcos High School. His team was discouraged, and the players drifted to the sidelines—except Brock. He walked straight to the center of the field and knelt—alone—to pray. He was there awhile, all alone, until a few Fallbrook FCA players joined him. God answered Brock's prayer.

What made him do it? Brock says, "I was always involved in my youth group—Teen Extreme, Student Venture—and I served in my church. But what helped me form a platform to reach my campus was Fellowship of Christian Athletes."

Brock hosted three team outreach pizza parties for the three teams he was captain of during his freshman year at SMHS. "I wanted to play sports, and I wanted to see if God would use sports to help reach people for Him. So when I went to SMHS as a freshman, I decided to host pizza parties to share my testimony and show a few clips of pro athletes. I wanted to then share the gospel message as clearly as possible." As a result of the three parties, more than thirty-four athlete friends had come to Christ.

Brock gives his mother's prayers credit for his success too. "Yesterday, when all the moms in Moms in Touch prayed, I realized the power of praying moms. As I looked at the other graduates, I saw that these moms had prayed us through. They prayed for me as I founded the FCA club; they prayed for all of us, and we all made it through strong. It was as if a force field was around us and Satan couldn't get to us!"

Brock was given the Athlete of the Year award for being a 4.0 scholar athlete, playing three sports, and breaking two school passing records. He was also awarded many scholarships, including one from the Retired NFL Players. In addition, at the San Marcos Senior Awards ceremony, Brock was given the Knight of the Year award—the highest one given at San Marcos High, voted on by faculty. When he was handed the award, the faculty rose to their feet and gave him a standing ovation. That same spring, he was presented with San Diego's Finest Citizen Award in front of a banquet audience of eight hundred. What was Brock's response?

"First, I want to thank my Lord and Savior, Jesus Christ. He died for me; I want to live for Him."

—Brock's story, as told by Pam Farrel

YB Young Believer

Young Believer Connection

Check out the I Believe statement "God hears and answers prayer" on page 1375 of the *Young Believer Bible.* Even Jesus prayed to his heavenly Father—and prayed for *us!*

READ: John 17

Think about It!

Think about a time when God clearly answered your prayer. When can you take a moment to give him thanks?

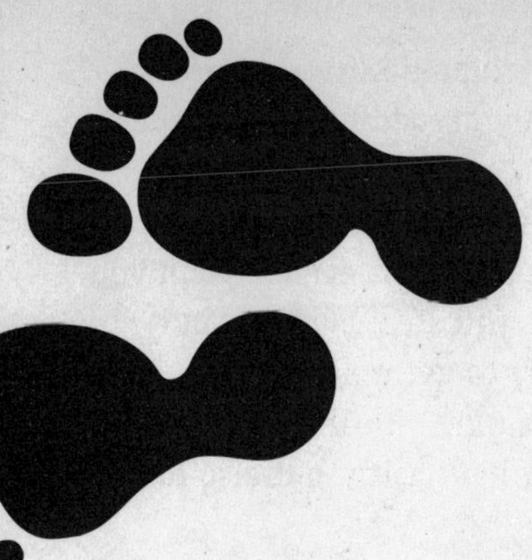

Breana's Brave Battle

FOCUSING IN

"I want to play. I will play. . . . And please . . . don't let my hair fall off!"

—Breana, age 15

"What do you mean, I have cancer?" said Breana. "I'm only thirteen! I can't have cancer."

Breana Scheppmann could see the doctor's mouth moving, yet she only heard a buzzing in her head as she tried to make sense of it all.

The doctor continued to explain. "Breana, the small lump on your shoulder is not a volleyball injury; it's a rare cancer that strikes young people. You're going to need some aggressive treatment." As the doctor turned toward her parents, Breana heard him drone on about "chemotherapy, surgeries, radiation . . ."

"What about volleyball? Can I still play volleyball?" Breana interrupted.

"I'm sorry. What?"

"Can I play volleyball in the fall?"

You see, God had designed Breana for volleyball. With her tall, slender frame, she could slam a serve over the net better than anyone on her team. Her quiet nature erupted into competitive fierceness on the court. Her school team needed her; she needed them.

"Well . . . ," the doctor said, hesitating. "I don't think you'll *want* to play much of anything. You're sick now, even though you don't feel it much. And the treatments will steal most of your strength. You need to save your energy to get well."

"I want to play. I *will* play," she argued. Breana sensed a battle was about to begin, not only for her health, but also for her beloved volleyball.

The ordeal of treatments began. Breana submitted herself first to one surgery to remove the tumor, and then to another that inserted a port for powerful medicine to flow directly into her body. She endured grueling rounds of chemotherapy. As the cancer-killing chemicals dripped into her body, she prayed for God to give her strength to continue. "God, please keep me brave. I feel so scared."

Although she didn't feel great, she knew God was helping her cope, one day at a time. New dilemmas arose each day as questions came from all directions. . . .

Which arm should we take blood from, Breana?

"Not my right arm! I serve the ball with that one!"

What type of wig do you want to cover your balding head?

"Let's go short and blond. It will be cute, and I won't worry about the hair straying into my eyes on the court. I just hope the whole thing doesn't tumble off!"

As volleyball season approached, Breana practiced and prayed. She practiced her serve; she prayed for strength. She practiced her jumps; she prayed her hair would stay on. She practiced her blocks; she prayed she could play when the season started.

One evening at church, Breana asked her youth group to pray

about her next doctor's visit. She explained that at the next appointment it would be decided whether she could participate in the volleyball games. The group huddled close, held hands, and prayed. Breana felt a new confidence as they brought their request to God.

Marching into the doctor's office, Breana bravely asked, "Doctor, would you like to come to my game this weekend?"

"What game are you talking about?" he responded, slightly confused.

"My first volleyball game of the season!"

"Well, yes, I would love to. What time does it start?"

"Does that mean I can play?" Breana said excitedly.

"Yes. You've faced more challenges in the last few months than most grown-ups ever do. After all the stuff I've put you through, I think you can handle a volleyball game or two. Now, what time does the game start?"

Game night finally arrived. Before entering the gym, Breana whispered, "God, you helped me get here. Now give me strength to serve the ball hard. And please . . . don't let my hair fall off!"

—Breana's story, as told by Susanne Scheppmann

Young Believer Connection

YB Young Believer

Check out the character study of the sick man who stayed by the pool of Bethesda on page 1355 of the *Young Believer Bible*. He needed physical healing too.

READ: John 5:1-15

Think about It!

How do you handle it when you are suffering physically? Can you keep a positive attitude and maintain your faith in God?

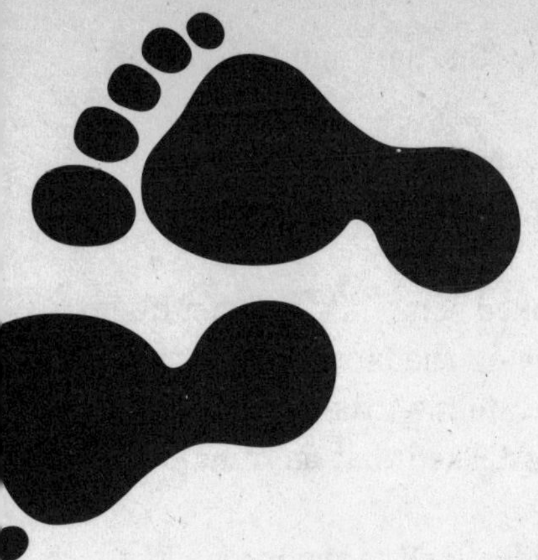

Help, One Cookie at a Time

FOCUSING IN

"Dear God . . . could you send some healing down to those left here who aren't feeling so happy?"

—Abby, age 8

Eight-year-old Abby Pitner smoothed her fingers across the pictures on her poster board, making sure the corners were securely glued down. As her eyes scanned each picture, she thought of the fun she'd had in New York City only days before.

"We're ready for you now," her teacher said.

Abby smiled and made her way to the front of the classroom. It was time to give her report about her trip to the city. Abby pointed to each picture on her poster board, sharing interesting facts and statistics about the marvelous structures in Manhattan.

"This is my favorite," she beamed, pointing to the World Trade Center buildings at the heart of her display. "They're so beautiful and tall!"

Just then a messenger from the school office opened the door to the classroom and interrupted Abby's report. He whispered something to her teacher, who gasped, "Oh, no!" and turned her face away from the children.

Patiently Abby waited for her teacher's signal to finish her report. Instead she was quietly told she could finish her report another day.

The teacher stood slowly and looked across a classroom filled with wide-eyed third-graders. The date on the large classroom calendar read, "September 11, 2001." Carefully, the teacher explained that the country had been attacked that morning in Washington and New York.

Abby's heart froze with fear. Suddenly she announced, "My daddy is in New York today."

The teacher nodded and said, "Yes, but your father's okay. Your mother sent word that he was nowhere near the World Trade Center at the time of the attack. He's fine, sweetie."

Abby sighed with relief, but she still felt upset. She stared at her photo of the Twin Towers, the shot she had taken with her disposable camera just days before.

Suddenly her home in Brandon, Florida, seemed very close to New York. Abby felt so connected to the city and its people. She couldn't stop wondering how many people died when the planes hit and the towers fell. How could those huge buildings disappear so quickly?

After school Abby sat close to her mother on the couch in their bright family room and watched as live news broadcasts switched between Washington, Pennsylvania, and New York. They saw family and friends of the missing hold up photos for the news cameras, expressing hope for their loved ones' survival.

That night when Abby knelt by her bedside, she prayed, "Dear God, I know you are excited to have more of your children on your lap tonight. Please give them a hug right now and let them know we care. I'm glad that you have your children there, but they left some people here who are really missing them. Could you send some healing down to those left here who aren't feeling so happy? Thanks a lot. Amen."

Later that week, as newscasts replaced regular programming, Abby and her sister, Alix, baked chocolate chip cookies to cheer up the family. As soon as they tasted the first warm samples, Abby realized how she could help the people in New York City.

"Mom! Dad! I know what we can do to help! Alix and I can bake a whole bunch of cookies and sell them," Abby explained. "Then we can give that money to the Red Cross to help the people in New York."

After a family discussion, the team made a decision based on the old truth that "You get by giving." Instead of selling the cookies, they decided to give them away. In return, Abby and her family requested that people go on-line and donate money to a participating charity.

But where could they direct the people to the charities? Her dad had the answer. His employer had moved quickly in the two days following the September 11 tragedy to create a Web site that enabled charities with no Internet site to receive donations on-line. That meant people could easily pick out charities listed on that one Web site. Abby's idea could really work!

So the Pitner family cookie crusade began. They baked hundreds of cookies. They decorated hundreds of goody bags with red, white, and blue stars, ribbons, and flags. And they passed out the bags all over their neighborhood and at a local bookstore.

"This is our gift to you," Abby's little sister said, grinning as she handed out each bag. "We hope you enjoy the goodies." When people opened the bag, they found the girls' delicious home-baked cookies and this note with the Web site address:

Dear Neighbor,

Please accept this gift and enjoy the goodies included. Last week our daughters, Abby, 7, and Alix, 5, had an idea to bake cookies and sell them to our neighbors to raise money for the Red Cross. The girls even came up with this pledge:

In God we trust.
We give our heart.
For those in need
We'll do our part.

Together, we decided that we would give the cookies away to our friends and neighbors with this note. While you're enjoying our gift, we hope you will go on-line to make a donation to one of the participating charities.

Whether or not you choose to contribute, please enjoy the goodies. And God bless.

The Pitners

Abby's patriotic giveaway caught the attention of a local TV station. In only a few weeks, the Pitner sisters' efforts made a huge impact, raising close to six thousand dollars.

Abby was happy to do her part. She says, "I learned that even if you're really small, you can still make a big difference."

—Abby's story, as told by Michelle Medlock Adams

YB Young Believer

Young Believer Connection

Check out the character study of the poor widow on page 1286 of the *Young Believer Bible.* This lady was small in wealth but large in giving. Remind you of anyone?

READ: Mark 12:41-44; Acts 20:35

Think about It!

When have you learned that "it is more blessed to give than to receive"? Spend a few moments recalling the warm feeling it gave you to give. What will be your next opportunity to enjoy that feeling again?

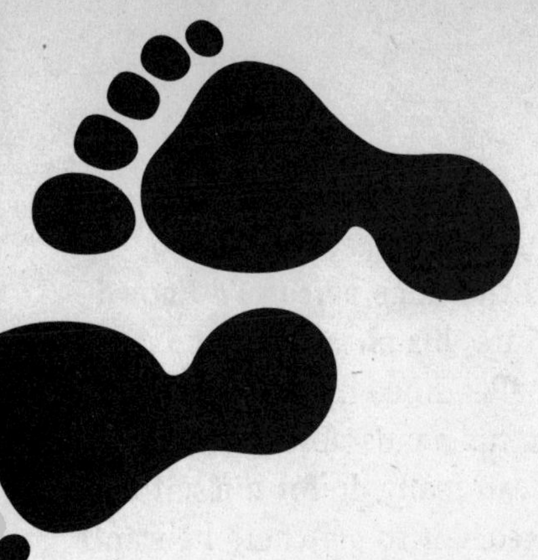

My Friend Sammy—Still the Same

FOCUSING IN

"It's the size of your heart that matters most."

—Daniel, age 16

Standing at five feet, four inches tall and weighing only 135 pounds, Sammy Hughes was not your average All-Conference high school football player. While some rely on brute strength, physical size, or lightning speed to help them bring down ball carriers, Sammy relied on pure heart and an unshakeable will to win. Though most of the other players were bigger and taller than Sammy, no one could match his enthusiasm and love for the game of football.

So I wasn't surprised by the reaction I witnessed from our team and the crowd as Sammy lay on the field with a paralyzing neck injury. We all stared in disbelief as a helicopter airlifted him off the football field that Friday night, never to walk again. Needless to say, the incident took all of the life out of our team as we dropped the next four games in a row. The game that once brought Sammy so much joy has confined him to a wheelchair—maybe for the rest of his life.

When I saw Sammy a while later, after months of hospital care, he was so different—but really, he was just the same. I'm talking about his inner spirit. Sammy was still the same person I'd known and played ball with for three years. Sure, his physical body is a lot different. His legs and arms are smaller since his muscles lost tone. He needs to have some straps on his hands now to keep them straight. And the only thing he can really do for himself is push the button on his motorized wheelchair to go where he wants to go.

And it hurts me to remember how much joy Sammy once got from his athletic ability. I think about all the times when he dove with reckless abandon into the legs of some tight end twice his size, some giant rumbling at him full speed. Sammy really loved to take down the biggest guys; he'd hit them low, and they'd always fall. But somehow, on that last hit, Sammy's head bent forward instead of backward. And something snapped.

But life didn't end at the end of his spinal cord. You see, the best and the most lasting thing I learned from Sammy is that physical size isn't the most important thing on the football field, or anywhere else: It's the size of your heart that matters most. No amount of physical strength guarantees you the courage to live life in a way that inspires everyone who knows you.

If you ask me, nobody has more guts than my friend Sammy. Now I look forward to the many other things he's going to teach me as he learns to deal with this challenge that God has allowed him to face.

—Daniel Wilde

YB Young Believer

Young Believer Connection

Check out the story of Mephibosheth on page 413 of the *Young Believer Bible*. He had crippled feet, but he was greatly beloved—even by the king of Israel.

READ: 2 Samuel 9:1-13

Think about It!

How do you define "courage"? Who, in your world, has the most guts?

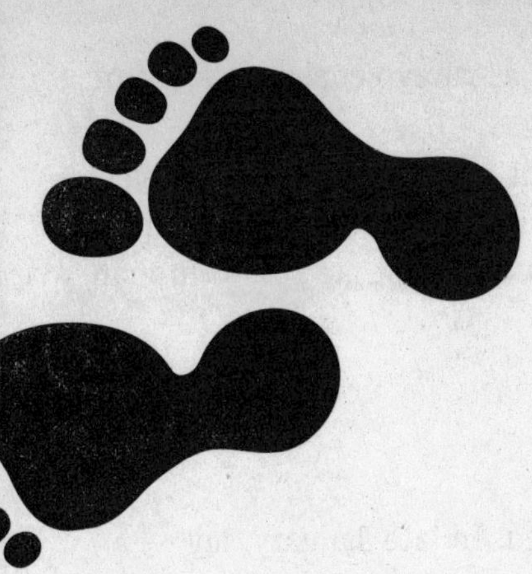

He Will Fill You

FOCUSING IN

"'Everybody goes through this,' they said. 'You just have to find yourself.' . . . But what did that mean?"

—Janelle, age 17

"Crybaby! Nobody likes a crybaby. . . ." The kids would tease me every time my eyes filled with tears. Unfortunately, my feelings were so sensitive that if anyone said one negative thing toward me, I would cry. Soon this response grew into something that was so instantaneous that I didn't know how to control it.

As you can imagine, an overweight, shy eleven-year-old crying at least one time a week didn't go over too well with the other kids. Not a day of school went by without somebody tormenting me about my watering eyes. I turned to my church youth group for help. In fact, going to youth group became the highlight of my week—and the only place I felt I could ever be myself. Near the end of sixth grade, I prayed to God that my "crying habit" would break . . . and it decreased a lot.

But all the rejection actually affected my relationships with people later on in life. This showed through especially in seventh grade because I was constantly trying to please the other kids. As a result, I became a big pushover. Not as many people made fun of me, but it still happened.

As my church became smaller that year (due to a pastor leaving), my youth group quickly became smaller too. But I developed bonds with friends in the youth group that kept me going through that year.

Then something truly terrible happened. In late January, my brother became paralyzed in a car accident that injured his spinal cord. At first, I went into a state of denial. *Nothing like this can happen to my family,* I thought. *My parents serve on the pastoral staff of our church!*

"We're good people—we don't deserve this!" I protested to God.

Soon I fell into depression and skipped school a bunch, thinking I was always sick. My grades dropped, and I lost a lot of weight. I leaned toward my church more than ever, but I discovered later that I didn't actually have a relationship with Jesus Christ—just with the church!

Eighth grade came, and I decided to avoid people. I felt so paranoid that I hardly ever spoke to anyone unless they spoke to me. Even though I continued going to church and youth group every week, I felt myself growing farther and farther away from God.

High school offered me a new start, and I felt some relief when kids seemed to like me. I even had my first boyfriend and went to homecoming. But at church the youth group was practically gone; I had only one good friend left.

As the year went on, I felt a lot of emotional instability. I would have panic attacks—mostly just slight ones that made my fingers tremble sometimes when I worked on an assignment.

One time in gym class, I was feeling particularly shaky when my PE teacher told me to get up and play basketball with the rest of the class. I said no, and then I blew up at her, shaking and crying uncontrollably. My teacher saw that I was not quite stable and got the school nurse while one of my friends tried to comfort me.

I had not cried the whole school year, and immediate flashbacks to sixth grade flooded my mind. I panicked even more: *What if I can't stop crying?* My mom picked me up from school right away and took me to a doctor. He said that I wasn't crazy or anything, which is what I feared, but he suggested doing some tests for mental illnesses.

Then later on in the school year, I felt intense emptiness that I had never felt before. I confided in a few friends about my feelings, and they told me that "everybody goes through this." They said I just needed to "find myself."

Find myself? What did that mean?

I wasn't sure. I even started praying about it, but it didn't seem to take me anywhere. Yet God heard my cries for help and prepared my heart for His answer.

That summer, I went to Young Life camp. I was very excited about it because I had been there before in junior high, and it had been the highlight of my year. But this time, one message at camp affected me spiritually in a way I had never felt before.

The illustration that caught my attention involved pouring different things into a glass. Every time the speaker poured something into a glass with holes, it remained empty. Then he poured water that represented Jesus into a glass without holes, and it filled right up.

This was a picture of my life. No matter what I put my time into, nothing could fill me up . . . nothing, that is, but Jesus. I asked Him into my life to save me and to fill up my emptiness.

But I still felt afraid. Many times before, I had gone on youth retreats and decided to live my life for God, then had come home and been the same person I was before. But even though I felt sick with a cold when I came home this time from camp, the first thing I did was to read my Bible.

For over a year now, I've been building my relationship with Jesus Christ. I still feel like a baby Christian. But my life has changed in many significant ways. Toward the middle of the school year, God helped me see the world in a whole new light.

No longer do I care what people think of me—it doesn't matter! The only thing that really matters is what God counts for eternity in heaven.

So despite my failures, I've been happier than I've been for years. All because I let Jesus come into my life and fill me up.

—Janelle Esposito

Young Believer Connection

YB Young Believer

Check out the character study of Hannah on page 358 of the *Young Believer Bible*. She was teased into tears—but God answered her prayers!

READ: 1 Samuel 1:1–2:1; Romans 8:31-34

Think about It!

When was the last time kids made fun of you? How much did it matter?

¤ It was the most important thing in my life.
¤ It made me feel bad, but I went on with my life.
¤ I didn't like it . . . but Christ is my life!

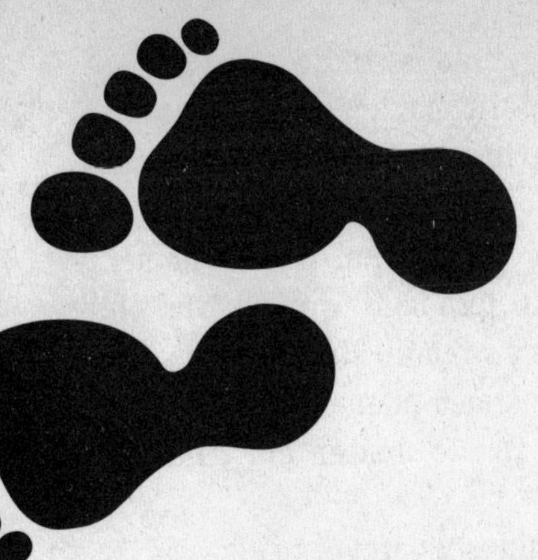

From Promise to Fulfillment

FOCUSING IN

"There are things I can't control, but God has a plan for them."

—Meghan, age 23

Meghan Moran could be working in a high-tech lab or in a comfortable corporate office, earning a good salary. Instead, she decided after graduating from college last year to keep a childhood promise to herself.

"In the first grade, one of my teachers went to Sierra Leone on a mission trip," Moran, 23, recalled recently. "A fourth-grade substitute teacher had been to Belize. I decided as a seventh-grader that I wanted to do the same thing." That promise led her to turn down two job offers—one a $40,000-a-year chemist position and the other a director position with a well-known nonprofit company. Moran's friends and family questioned her decision, but she was certain that joining the Jesuit Volunteer Corps for a year was part of her purpose.

"No one can get over the fact that I'm doing this," said Moran, who is the youngest of four children. "I did it to remind myself how much I've been given." She graduated with a degree in biology and another in theology and religious studies. She also earned minors in chemistry and nonprofit management. Meghan was prepared to serve some of the metro area's neediest citizens: homeless children.

Moran works at a nonprofit organization that provides emergency and transitional housing to homeless men, women, and children. As a child advocate at the agency's family shelter, she serves as a case manager for four families. She also plans recreational activities for all of the children living in the shelter and arranges for volunteers to visit the youths.

On many days, Moran simply handles whatever needs arise. She serves meals, answers the telephone, cleans the agency's third-floor office and supply closet, oversees residents' chores, and takes them to appointments or job interviews. Her workdays sometimes get long, but she doesn't mind.

"To see someone who was so broken inside when they got here be able to turn around—that's impressive," Moran said. The support she's offering homeless women and children is also impressive, says the director of the organization where Meghan works. "We're so lucky to have her," the director added. "She works with the children nonstop. In fact, we have to tell her not to come in on the weekends because she's doing so much."

Moran and three other volunteers receive $332 each month. After she pays her portion of rent and utilities for the house they share, Moran has about $85 left. "If you think about it, a lot of people on welfare live on this each month," she said. "It teaches you to prioritize."

Prioritizing has been key to getting—and giving—the most from this experience, she said. "I've had kids get into fights and [once] a lady yelled at me for something I didn't do, but it's worth it," she said.

Moran, whose interests range from medicine and public health to social work and fund-raising, hasn't decided what she'll do when she completes her volunteer experience. For now, she's content to live in the moment. "My faith grounds me a lot," she said. "It reminds me that there are things I can't control, but God has a plan for them. This experience has made me more aware of things I can do in the world. I'm giving a part of me to whomever I can touch. It may not mean a monumental change to their lives, but at least I'm doing something."

—Meghan's story, as told by Stacy Hawkins Adams

YB Young Believer

Young Believer Connection

Check out the character study of Samuel on page 361 of the *Young Believer Bible.* As a young child, Samuel was called to do God's work by serving as a priest in the temple. His childhood promise and potential came true in his adult life.

READ: 1 Samuel 3:1-21

Think about It!

When have you sensed God calling you to do work for him? Was it a long time ago? recently? Or are you still listening with an open heart for his guidance?

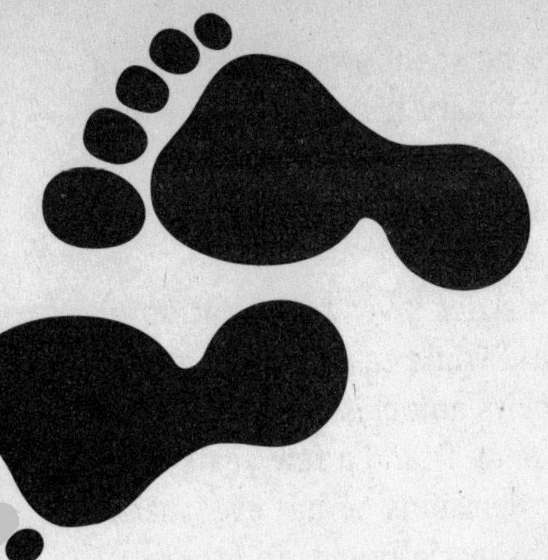

Now You're Cooking!

FOCUSING IN

"Ever since I was little, I've been interested in cooking."
—Sean, age 16

Being part of a cooking class doesn't make Odenton, Ohio, teenager Sean Broadwick feel odd or less masculine than his peers. In fact, being around a bunch of guys is what he expected when he signed up for the culinary arts class at the Center of Applied Technology North, a vocational trade school in Severn, Maryland. "Ever since I was little, I've been interested in cooking," Sean said. "Cooking is perceived to be a woman's job, but if you look at the chef industry as a whole, there's a majority of guys in it."

A junior at Arundel High in Gambrills, Ohio, Sean said cooking is more than learning recipes. It's also about safety, cleanliness, and being able to learn different cooking techniques. "I haven't really thought about what type of chef I would like to be yet," the sixteen-year-old said, sautéing onions for a spinach-and-mushroom Alfredo lasagna he was helping to prepare. "I don't want to do anything too high-end, but something where I could try a lot of different things."

For the past two summers, Sean has been doing new things in

and out of the classroom. Last summer he spent a month traveling in Kenya and southern Africa on a missionary trip with Teen Mania Ministries, a Texas-based Christian youth organization. The summer before that, he spent two weeks with the group in Caracas, Venezuela.

Founded in 1987, Teen Mania Ministries gives teens nationwide the opportunity to travel the world while teaching people in other countries about Christ through skits and classroom seminars. Sean first heard of the organization from a friend a few years ago and said joining it was one of the best decisions he has ever made. "It breaks my heart to see how people, especially kids in other countries, live," he said. "We try to talk to as many people as we can, but we also try to learn ourselves."

Part of a group of twenty-five teenagers, Sean raised a lot of the four thousand dollars necessary to go to Africa. "I got a lot of family and friends to donate some money, but I saved up a lot from my job and tax returns," he said. It took Sean more than six months to raise the money, but he said it was well spent. "Learning the culture was an awesome experience," he said. "The kids there made the trip most worthwhile. We ended up giving away a lot of our clothes and stuff because they had so little, and we had so much to come back to."

Those who know Sean said he shows as much conviction in everything he does. "He's very active in both this school and his other one," said Bruce Davis, a culinary arts teacher at CAT North. "He's very professional in what he does, and his experience last summer allows him to bring a capable leadership to the class."

—Sean's story, as told by Paul Wilson

Young Believer Connection

Check out the I Believe statement "God chose people to share his message" on page 792 of the *Young Believer Bible.*

READ: Psalm 96:2-3

Think about It!

List some of the talents and abilities God can use to spread the word about Jesus. Think: What are my own special abilities? Have I given them to the Lord?

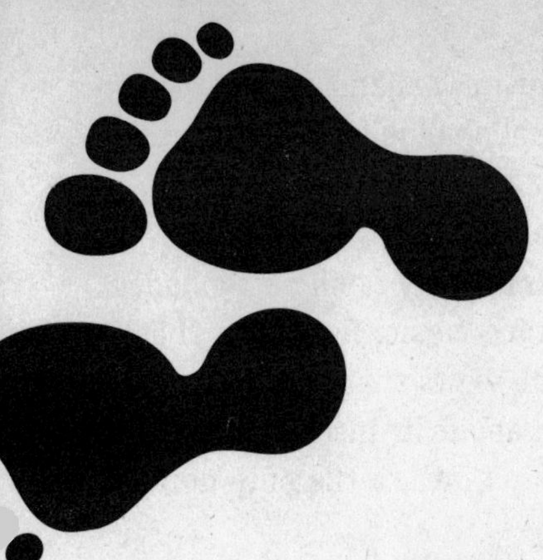

When Belief Just Stops

FOCUSING IN

"I had everybody fooled . . . but I'd stopped believing in the power of God."

—Nick, age 15

No, I never did drugs or anything like that. But in spite of seeming like a good Christian on the outside, I was spiritually dead and full of unbelief on the inside. Yep, I had everybody fooled, except God.

You see, I like to tell people I was born in Sunday school—popped out wearing a three-piece suit and toting a *Baby's First Bible* (which, I'm happy to report, I still have tucked away in my room).

My mom taught Sunday school. As some of you may know, when you're a little kid and your mom teaches Sunday school, it practically guarantees that you're going to hear about Jesus early in your life. What it doesn't guarantee, however, is that you accept Jesus as your Savior or live like a Christian once you've grown up.

On the other hand, my dad worked for the government and traveled around the world. So the summer before my third-grade year, we packed up and moved to Thailand—my first experience of a culture that didn't believe in Christianity. That's not when I began to doubt, though. My time spent in Thailand only helped to show me more about the world. The real change came three years later, when my family moved from Thailand to a small air force base in North Hampton, England.

On the base was a small chapel, which my family attended. It was a nice little church, nice people, nice music. But about that time in my life, I began to question the views that had been passed down to me. I didn't talk much about it; instead I kept my questions to myself, partly because of my father, the only non-Christian member in my family.

See, from the time I was in Thailand to the time I lived in England, I remember praying in church service after church service, "God, make my dad come to church. If he would only go to church, then he could get saved and everything in our family would be perfect."

One Sunday God honored my prayer. My dad decided that he was going to go to church with us. I had never seen my father in church, and I was very excited. I knew that once he was there, he'd find salvation and everything would turn out great in our home.

Well, halfway through the service Dad got up and left. When we got home, we found him on the couch watching football and complaining that we took too long getting back.

I realized that even though my dad went to church, he wasn't saved. And it was in that small moment that I stopped believing in the power of God.

During those four years when I was in England, my disbelief in God's power slowly turned to disbelief in God himself. I wasn't an atheist, exactly. I knew God existed, but I had no belief in Him. The weird thing is, it didn't stop me from going to church.

I just began "playing the game," as I've heard some Christians call it. Well, I became the ultimate game player—went to church, bowed my head in prayer, led a Vacation Bible School class, even participated in communion. No one suspected that I had turned my back on God.

Then, after four years in England, the time came for my family to finally go back to the USA. So we moved back to my hometown of Manassas, Virginia, and for some reason I wanted to keep going to church. I don't know why. Looking back, I'd like to say God was tugging at my heart, or that I wanted to get my life right with "the powers that be." But to be honest, I was just trying to keep up the show of being a Christian.

So I went to a youth group called Firepower near where I lived. For three Wednesdays in a row I sat unmoved throughout the service. Finally, when the fourth week came, I was ready to totally give up. It had gotten boring, and I didn't want to play anymore. I made up my mind that I wasn't coming back at all after that night.

That night I again sat unmoved through the worship, the sermon, and the pastor's call to pray at the front altar. But something happened when I got up to leave. I accidentally bumped into a youth leader named James. After a little small talk, he asked if he could pray with me. So, wanting to keep up my little act, I said, "Sure." He pointed to the front, and down we went.

What happened next was totally mind-blowing for me. James put his hands on my shoulders and started to pray. What he said was totally amazing, because he prayed for everything I was thinking about!

I'm serious.

All of a sudden I felt what I can only describe as the power of God hit and drop me to my knees. I can't explain why, but I started crying. James continued praying for me, and I can only say that something very strange happened deep in my soul. There was this warmth over my entire body, and I realized God was trying to get my attention. (You probably figured that out, right?)

Anyway, that night I gave my life back to God.

Has everything been wonderful since then? No way. In fact, I seem to have more problems than ever. But you know what else I have?

The *power* of God.

—Nick Clark

YB Young Believer

Young Believer Connection

Check out the character study of the prophet Habakkuk on page 1172 of the *Young Believer Bible.* He struggled with why God's power didn't seem to kick in when he wanted it to.

READ: Habakkuk 1–3

Think about It!

Think about a time when God's power seemed most present or most absent to you. What would you like to say to God about this?

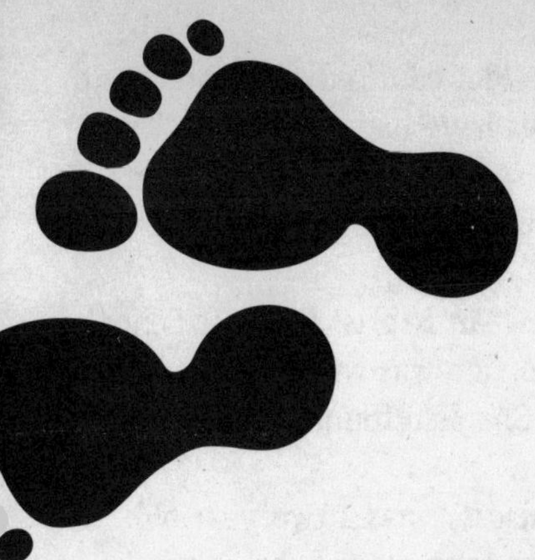

Youth Can March, Too

FOCUSING IN

"The unborn child didn't get a chance."

—Michele, age 14

Thirty years after the Supreme Court declared abortion legal, a new generation joined the picket line to protest a decision that still ignites passions across the country. Teens and even elementary school children listening to members of Congress address the crowd spoke with the same angst that has marked the debate since *Roe v. Wade* became the law of the land on January 22, 1973.

"I think abortion is one of the things out there that our generation should fight for," said Drew Phillips, 17, from northeast Maryland. He wondered about society's loss if potential geniuses were aborted. "Abortion should be outlawed," he said.

Phillips also said, "One of my best friends had [an abortion], and I don't hold it against her. Everyone's opinion and choice is up to them, but you have to think of the morality of the situation . . . the morality causes us to disagree, but you always have to love the sinner, not the sin." Phillips hopes to become a brother in the Catholic church one day.

His classmate Dana Blackwelder, 17, said she is against abortion because she was adopted. Blackwelder counted three pregnant friends and said some of her classmates have had abortions. "We don't talk about it. We pretty much respect each other's opinions," she said. Today's protest was the fourth time she has attended the annual event.

Blaire Ogarrogreene, 17, from St. Jean Baptist Catholic School in New York City, said she realized abortion was wrong when she learned about the medical procedure. She also found out the issue can be complicated.

She said one of her classmates, also 17, has a two-year-old. "She still goes to school, but she has to take care of the baby. She's working at the same time. She doesn't hang out so much." When asked what she thought about her friend's choice, Ogarrogreene said, "She loves her daughter. It's not the baby's fault. I'd take the responsibility."

What does she think the government should do? "Everyone has the right to their own opinion. To be honest, I think the government shouldn't step in," she said. "It should be a choice of every individual." Still, she said people shouldn't get abortions. "Taking someone's life is the cowardly way," she said. "I really hope we make a difference here today."

Christian Senner, a 21-year-old Georgetown University student, said, "The existence of abortion means that we're not doing enough to help women. If women want to have abortions, we have to enable them to do what they want. As it stands, there are three options: one, carrying to term; two, adoption; three, abortion. We have to enable women to choose between one and two. . . . Some choices are wrong."

"It's against my religion. . . . The unborn child didn't get a chance," said Michele Diamond, 14, from Pennsylvania. Diamond and her classmates at Nativity of Our Lord Catholic School recently wrote essays about why they were pro-life. Most of the seventh- and eighth-grade students from her school attended the protest. Students said those who didn't attend the protest were marked absent for the day.

One 12-year-old said her older sister had recently had an abortion against her family's wishes. "It was kind of scary. She cried a lot because she regretted it."

Erika Deniger, 15, was at the rally with sister Joy, 13. "I've been involved since I was born," Erika said, "and anyone under 30 has been involved, because they survived."

—Michele's story, as told by Liz Fox and Lydia McCoy

Young Believer Connection

YB Young Believer

Check out the character study of Caleb on page 194 and the key verse on page 298 of the *Young Believer Bible*. Caleb followed and spoke up for God completely, even when the other spies didn't.

READ: Numbers 13–14; Joshua 14:8

Think about It!

What issue in society today seems most important to you? How bold are you in speaking up for God's truth about this?

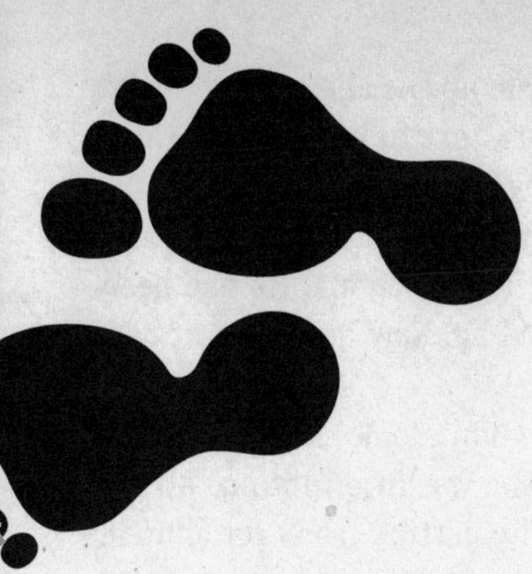

Want to Help?

FOCUSING IN

Did he really mean that? He wanted her help with . . . praying?

—Meghan, age 11

Meghan groaned as she walked through the doors of church that Sunday morning. She had forgotten her book again! Now she would have to wait the whole hour before worship—with nothing to do—while her parents rushed around getting ready with all the other grown-ups. Even some of the older kids had jobs to do, like helping with the sound system. What was she going to do?

It wasn't that Meghan minded being in church. In fact, she enjoyed Sunday worship. Her father was the pastor of the church, while her mother helped lead the worship team. It was just that every Sunday, Meghan's family was often the first to arrive in the building and sometimes the last to leave. Everyone bustled around—setting up tables, putting out coffee and donuts, hooking up microphones, and practicing music. But there weren't many jobs for a kid to do.

Meghan wandered down the hall to the Sunday school class-rooms. She remembered that her class had made collages last week. Maybe her teacher had hung them up. As she walked down the hall, she glanced into the classroom next to hers. Out of the corner of her eye she saw someone move. She froze.

"Oh. Hi, Tom," she said. Standing in the corner of the classroom was the director of the Sunday school program. He had been staring off into space as Meghan walked by. Now he smiled at her.

"Hi, Meghan."

Meghan hesitated by the door. It didn't look like he was busy doing anything, but she still felt like she was interrupting. All the other adults were rushing around, busily getting ready for church. What was Tom doing?

She asked him.

"Well," he said slowly. "I'm praying for this Sunday school class."

There was a pause.

"Do you want to help?" he added. Meghan blinked. Did he really mean that? He wanted her help with . . . *praying?*

"Sure!" she said. She suddenly felt excited. Finally there was something she could do! "What do you do?" she added.

"Well, I go from classroom to classroom praying for each teacher and each student. How about you praying for your own class in the room next door?"

They walked down the hall into Meghan's room. Sure enough, there were the collages from last week and Bible-verse posters taped up around the walls. Meghan sat down at the table. It suddenly occurred to her that she didn't know what to pray about.

"Tom?" she called as he started to leave the room. "What should I pray for?"

He thought about that for a moment. "I guess you could pray that the students would learn what they're supposed to learn today," he said. Then he left.

Meghan folded her hands and closed her eyes. "Good morning, God," she said. "I've been given a special job this morning. . . ."

A few minutes later, Tom walked by the classroom where he had sent Meghan to pray. He had been to all the classrooms, praying for each teacher and each student. Hers was the only one left. He glanced in. There she was, still sitting at the table with her hands folded and her eyes squeezed tightly shut. He smiled. *No need for me to pray in there,* he thought. *It's covered.*

After Sunday school, Tom walked through the halls again. He helped some of the teachers straighten up their classrooms and checked that each visitor had had a good experience. Seeing Meghan's teacher, Nancy, he made a beeline for her classroom door.

"Hey, Nancy!" he said. "Did anything special happen in your class today?"

Nancy looked up in surprise, then paused to think.

"Well . . . yeah, now that you mention it. For some reason, the kids were especially attentive today. I think they really understood what I was teaching."

Tom nodded and smiled. "Want to know why?"

—Meghan's story, as told by Sarah Arthur

Young Believer Connection

Check out the character study of Nehemiah on page 644 of the *Young Believer Bible.* Nehemiah was a man who prayed constantly, about everything—especially that God would protect his people from enemies and from fighting among themselves.

READ: Nehemiah 1:1-11

Think about It!

Do you have a prayer list? Who are you praying for today?

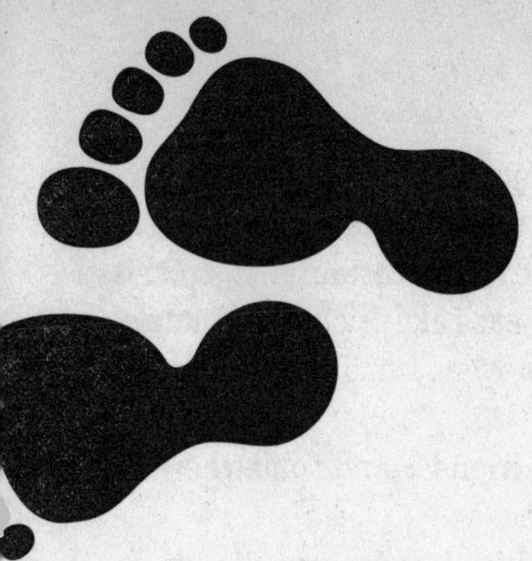

19 Without a Big Tree . . . Better!

FOCUSING IN

"If I had gotten the tree house like I wanted, would the club have taken off?"

—Vashti, age 10

"Well, Vashti, this is our new home. . . ."

That's what my mom said as I ran quickly through the house to see the backyard. It looked . . . okay. There was a nice flower bed and a few small trees, but the one thing I had hoped for was missing. More than anything, I wanted to build a treehouse and start a group for girls.

"I want to call it the 'Love God Club,'" I'd told my parents when we first heard that we were moving to a new community. This would give me an opportunity to be like my folks. "I want the girls to worship and read the Bible and pray, and have snacks and crafts and play games."

Now it looked like my dream would not happen, at least not in this backyard, which looked more like a cow pasture.

I was only seven when my dad took a job as worship pastor at a new church in upper Michigan. So we moved from a downtown historic district, with cute shops and friendly restaurants, to this sprawling Michigan farm community near Lake Michigan. I knew that life would be much different from what I had experienced before.

But I had a plan for making new friends! And somewhere I had to find a big tree for my tree house.

"Let's be thankful that we found this place for rent, Vashti. It took us a long time to find something. I know how much you wanted the tree house, but we'll find a place for your club. You'll see."

Of course, this wasn't the first time that my parents had gone along with my ideas for ministry. Back when I was four or five, if we passed an accident or a fire or something, I would beg my parents to pray with me for the people who were hurt. I didn't even wait for them to pray, I'd just begin.

That's how I think and feel. I love people, and I want them to love Jesus, like I do!

Soon after we moved into the new house and unpacked everything, my sister and I played in the big empty boxes in the garage. That's when I realized how we could make a clubhouse that wasn't in a big tree. Maybe all we needed was a tent for our club.

Well, that would work for the summertime, but if we put it inside the garage, then the club could meet anytime. We'd never have to worry about being too cold or too wet to meet. The kitchen door led right out to the garage, so we could come and go without even going outside!

I couldn't wait to get the word out that a new club would meet at our house as soon as we were ready. At first I invited the girls my own age that I'd met at our new church.

"What should our Bible study be about?" I asked my mom.

"Well, I think you should pray about it and let God tell you," she said.

That year, I prayed and asked God what to do—and He answered. I also prayed about what worship songs to sing, and my mom helped me buy notebooks and pencils for all the girls so they could write out prayer requests.

Even the snacks went along with the study themes for each day, and on the final day, snack time featured a big cake with JESUS spelled out in sprinkles on top.

My mom typed up a daily plan for me to follow, and supervised as my friends and I enjoyed the Love God Club.

Once we talked about the bride of Christ, and the girls created toilet-paper wedding dresses on each other. This year we read Esther and had the theme "Beautiful Inside and Out." Women from the church came and led sessions on bead making, hair care, and manners, and we ended with a Victorian tea.

I really like singing and dancing, so I added worship dance to our club activities. I helped choreograph a worship piece, and the group performed it in Kidz Planet, the Sunday morning kids' program at our church.

The Love God Club is now in its third year. Girls from many churches and backgrounds attend, including girls from public school, home school, and my dance classes. It's really fun. I like talking together and planning the big party that happens at the end every year.

But the thing I wonder about is, if I had gotten the tree house like I wanted, would the club have taken off like this? Or would I have just been content to enjoy the fun of a big tree with a few friends? Hey—God knows best!

—Vashti's story, as told by Jennie Bishop

Young Believer Connection

Check out the character study of Lydia on page 1417 of the *Young Believer Bible.* Lydia opened up her house to others too.

READ: Acts 16:14, 40

Think about It!

If you were to invite some new friends over to your room, would it be ready for visitors? Think: Right now, my room looks like . . .

¤ a tornado zone—"We have debris!"
¤ a cave—dark, dreary, and filled with creepy-crawlies.
¤ a little bit of heaven—all clean, bright, and light.

Remember: Real hospitality means being ready to welcome others with an encouraging smile and an open heart, no matter how grand or simple your home is.

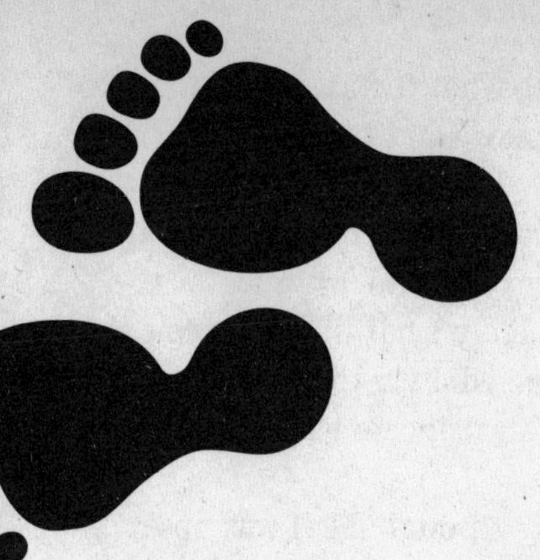

To Tell or Not to Tell

FOCUSING IN

"I'd tell you to do what you know is right even if it seems hard to do."

—MacKenzie, age 15

A sudden cold feeling of shock came over me even though it was a warm summer afternoon.

I was twelve that summer. We had moved to this community about six months earlier when my dad was called to be the pastor of a growing church. That particular day, Doug, our church's youth leader, needed a baby-sitter for a few hours, so I was going to baby-sit his two kids for him.

We were all feeling hot and sweaty, so before Doug left, the kids asked if we could all walk down the street to get some ice cream while he was gone.

Doug said, "Okay, sure. There's some money in a tin on the top shelf of the closet in my room. Just go in there and take what you need."

After he left, I went into the bedroom and opened the closet. I guess I picked up the wrong tin, because when I opened it I was totally surprised and shocked to find marijuana instead of money.

I could smell it, and I knew right away what it was. I just stood there with my mouth open. I didn't know what to think, or what I should do.

I remembered how Doug was always telling our youth group not to do drugs. We had even had a big "Say 'No' to Drugs" program just a few weeks earlier. Suddenly I felt like Doug was a big liar and a hypocrite. But then I immediately thought about how I'd always looked up to him and how sincere he had always seemed to be.

A million emotions were pumping through me. I was upset and torn between my thoughts about what I believed was wrong and my feelings of loyalty to someone I considered to be a leader and a friend. I didn't want to get Doug in trouble because he seemed to be a good youth leader, but I knew what he was doing wasn't right. I felt totally mixed up about what to do.

Almost two miserable weeks went by. Every day I felt worse and worse. I felt guilty about not telling anyone what I knew, but I just couldn't bring myself to tell the truth and maybe get Doug in a lot of trouble. I prayed over and over and asked God for the answer, but for a while I still didn't know what I should do.

Finally I told my friend, Sandy, what had happened. Sandy said, "I think you've just got to tell your dad." I believed she was right, but the thought of actually doing it was really hard for me. I liked Doug, and I liked his family. I prayed about the situation some more.

When I talk to God, which is pretty much all the time, He seems to give me little signs about what I should do. Sometimes, He gives me that little "knowing feeling" inside my heart about what's right or wrong. Now I said, "Oh, please, God, tell me what to do."

It seemed like God heard me and answered my prayer. I decided to tell my dad what had happened by writing the whole thing in a letter. Even though my dad and I are really close, this way seemed easier for me. I could explain it better in writing than I could by just saying the words. I went to the living room and gave him the letter. Then I sat there watching him while he read it. I felt so bad about it that I started crying while he was reading.

The next day, my dad called Doug into his office and talked to him. Later, I was shocked to find out Doug had resigned and he and his family were moving to Wisconsin. I was really sad about that, and I knew it was all my fault. I had felt guilty before because I hadn't spoken up, but now I felt twice as guilty because I had!

My dad could see that I was having a hard time with all this, so he talked to me and told me I had done the right thing. When I thought it over, I said, "Yeah, I did the right thing, but I still feel bad about it, and I probably always will."

To make matters worse, my friend Sandy was upset that Doug was leaving, and so she was mad at me. Sandy was the first friend I had made when we moved to this community. Even though she was the one who said I should tell my dad, she hadn't expected that Doug would leave. The main reason Sandy was mad at me was that she was "best buddies" with Doug's son, Zack—she really liked him a lot. They always hung out. Now Zack and his family had to move away and, of course, Sandy was blaming me.

It's been a few years since it happened, but I still feel guilty every time I think about Zack, even though I know I did what was right. Making the right choice and doing what God tells you to do is sometimes pretty hard. But when I think of what could have happened to some of the other kids, or to Doug's own kids—if he kept on being a youth leader and using illegal drugs—I just know I did what needed to be done.

I believe Doug probably learned a valuable lesson from this experience. I'm hoping so, and I'm pretty sure that this made him realize his mistake and want to change his actions.

I'm so grateful that I have a close relationship with both my parents. I thank God I can tell them what's bothering me. Most of my friends can't do that with their parents. I'm lucky.

If I were giving advice, I'd tell you to do what you know is right even if it seems hard to do. I'd tell you to find someone you can trust—a pastor, a good friend, or a grandparent—anyone who really cares about you, who cares about what's right, and who will listen. Talk things over with that person, but don't forget to pray too.

I think about what could have happened if someone other than me had found the pot. That person might have taken it and started experimenting with it. All kinds of bad things could have happened. When I think about that, I'm so glad I did the right thing. God was leading me and thankfully, I was listening.

God is always there for us. We just need to tell Him the problem and ask for His help.

—MacKenzie's story, as told by Diana L. James

Editor's Note: Except for the author's name, all names in this story have been changed.

Young Believer Connection

Check out the character study of Esther on page 670 of the *Young Believer Bible.* She also had to decide whether to tell the truth to someone in authority.

READ: Esther 4:16

Think about It!

Have you ever decided to "tell" on someone about something important? When is that the right thing to do?

21 Rachel's Joy

FOCUSING IN

"What I wouldn't give for a bowl of steaming rice!"

—Rachel, age 17

The church van pulled to a stop. Rachel gazed in dismay out the window. They had stopped in front of a dingy little Chinese restaurant somewhere on the south side of Chicago.

"Let's eat!" their trip leader said cheerfully as he opened the van doors. The high school youth group was starved after spending the whole day doing inner-city service projects. In Rachel's opinion, they deserved to eat at someplace cool—like the Hard Rock Cafe. But their youth leader insisted on stretching them out of their "comfort zones." This was going a little too far, though!

"I don't like Chinese food," Rachel whined.

Her trip leader raised an eyebrow. "Well, girl, this is all you've got."

Rachel climbed out of the van with a groan and followed her friends inside. Before long, plates of steaming hot food were being passed around. To Rachel's surprise, everyone dug in gratefully. Some were even attempting to use the chopsticks, which made the others laugh. After a few minutes Rachel asked for a small bowl of white rice. She picked at the rice and scowled for the rest of the meal. *How can they stand it?* she thought. *I could never do mission work like this all the time—and then eat rice for my dinner.* Little did she know what would come years later. . . .

"It's your turn to cook tonight, Blake—remember?"

"Dude, I forgot. What do we have left?" Blake wandered over to the fridge and peeked inside. Shaking his head, he went through cupboard after cupboard until he found the bag of apples.

"This is all we've got?" he said.

Rachel nodded. "We don't have any more money."

"Great," he replied sarcastically. He eyed the apples, then looked up and grinned. "There's only enough for each of us to have one. Shall I slice the apples up, just to make it look like more food?"

Rachel laughed, but was it really funny?

Three years had passed since Rachel's first trip to the south side of Chicago. The experience had haunted her all through high school. She had begun to pray that God would show her if he wanted her to do something like that again after graduation. Maybe she could even be a missionary! She had applied to one mission program and been accepted—but the trip had been canceled.

Then came Mission Year. Rachel had found out about the program through some friends. It required a year of service in an American city—in a part of the city that most people wouldn't go to. Volunteers lived in an inner-city house with five other young adults. Through participation in a local church, the ministry found ways to get to know the neighbors, which included spending twenty hours a week helping out somewhere in the community, such as a school or clinic. Like most missionaries, Rachel would have to raise money to cover the costs by asking for help from family and friends. It would be hard work!

Rachel had been excited as she filled out the application. "Which city would be your first choice?" the application asked. She wrote it out in capital letters: "C-H-I-C-A-G-O." It was months before she finally found out that she had gotten her first choice.

She and her teammates moved into the house in August. It took some time to get to know everybody. Not everyone got along right away—especially when it came to the chores. They all took turns with grocery shopping, cooking, and cleaning. But the toughest chore was making sure they had enough money to make it through each week. Rachel knew that the experience of eating only a slice of apple for a meal would teach them to manage their food funds better!

"Apples?" Rachel's teammates groaned.

Blake shrugged as they sat down to eat. "That's all we've got."

There was a brief silence as they looked dismally at their plates. Rachel couldn't help remembering that night so long ago at the Chinese restaurant. *What I wouldn't give for a bowl of steaming rice!* she thought. They had all worked so hard today—harder than she had worked at any youth group service project. Yet didn't the joy they had received from serving others make it all worth it?

"Well, who is going to say a prayer of thanks?" Blake asked.

No one spoke. There was an uncomfortable pause. Then finally Rachel raised her head with a smile.

—Rachel's story, as told by Sarah Arthur

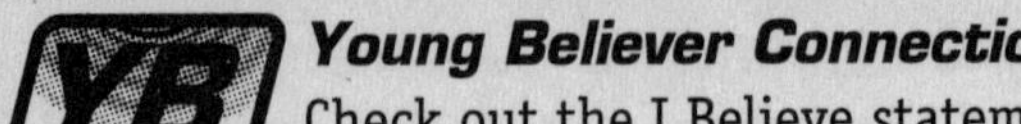

Young Believer Connection

Check out the I Believe statement "God is shaping me to be more like Jesus" on page 1524 of the *Young Believer Bible.* One of the ways God is changing each believer is to prepare him or her to be of service to others.

READ: Philippians 1:6

Think about It!

When is it easiest for you to complain? What helps you gain a better attitude?

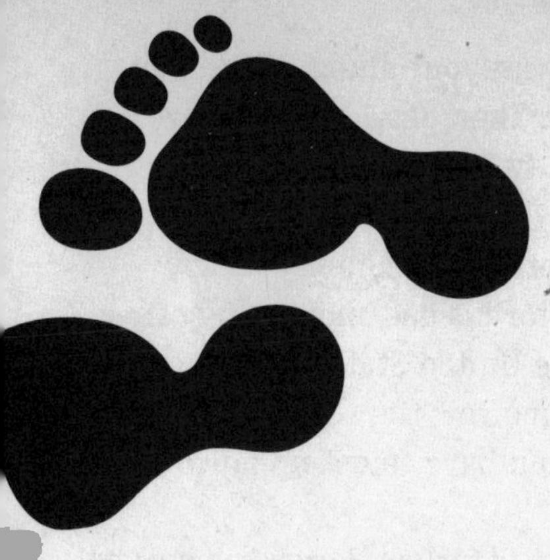

22 Sea Dad

FOCUSING IN

"Dad, I really missed you. . . . Weren't you scared and lonely?"

—Barry, age 8

Barry sat on the couch on his knees. His elbows were resting on the windowsill, his chin in his hands. He knew his dad wouldn't be home until tomorrow, but he was playing a game, pretending that today was the day. He imagined that if he stared out the window long enough and hard enough, his dad would walk up the driveway. Then he would rush out to meet him.

Mom walked into the room and saw Barry sitting there. "Oh, Barry, what are you doing? Your dinner is getting cold. I thought you said if I let you eat in here today you would watch your video and eat dinner."

"I know, Mom; I was just pretending that today was the day Dad would be home. I wish it could be today. Then I'd sit at the table and we'd tell Dad about how much we missed him, right?"

"Yes, honey, I wish it could be today too. It won't be until tomorrow, though, and we have to go pick Daddy up."

"Yeah, that's why I get to miss school!"

"Yes, but right now you need to eat your dinner. Then you need to finish picking up your things. Then get a bath and get some sleep so we can get up really early, okay?"

"Okay, Mom."

As his mom helped him say his prayers before bed, Barry remembered all the prayers he'd said for his dad since he'd been gone. Barry's dad was an officer in the United States Navy, and he'd been on a six-month mission. Tomorrow the ship would pull in at 8:30 A.M. Barry and his mom would have to get up much earlier.

The next day it was still dark outside when Barry's mom came into his room.

"Wake up, Barry. Today is the day," said Mom.

After he rubbed his eyes to get them to stay open, Barry got very excited. He had so much to tell his dad. He and his mom got ready and headed to the military base where the ship would come in. While they were waiting, Mom opened the breakfast they had bought. They talked about all the things they would tell Dad when they saw him.

Finally, the time came, and they spotted Dad coming down the walkway and making his way toward them. Barry ran up and gave his father a hug. Mom was only a second behind. They hugged for a long time. Suddenly Barry couldn't remember any of the things he wanted to tell his father. He was just glad that he was there. Dad knelt down to look Barry in the eye.

"Son, I missed you so much."

"Dad, I really missed you too, and I was worried about you. Weren't you scared and lonely?"

Dad smiled. "I was missing you both. Sometimes it was difficult, sometimes even a bit scary. But I was never alone. I knew you were praying for me. It felt lonely sometimes, yet I knew I wasn't alone."

"Because God was with you, right, Dad?"

"Yes, Barry, that's right. I thought of you and Mom and God a whole lot. I read my Bible and prayed for you both too. There is one passage that really gave me comfort. Would you like to hear it?"

"Sure, Dad."

"It's in Psalm 107:23-25. 'Some went off in ships, plying the trade routes of the world. They, too, observed the Lord's power in action, his impressive works on the deepest seas. He spoke, and the winds rose, stirring up the waves.'"

"Wow, that's neat, Dad. So you were reminded every day that God was with you! Isn't that great, Mom?"

"Yes, it is, Barry. Come on, let's head for home."

As they got into the car, Barry started to remember all the things he wanted to tell Dad about on the way home. Dad hardly got a word in edgewise.

—Barry's story, as told by Peter D. Mallett

Young Believer Connection

Check out the character study of Job on page 703 of the *Young Believer Bible.* Also see the I Believe statement "I grow stronger with God's help during tough times" on page 714.

READ: Job 42:12-17

Think about It!

Are you able to believe that God is with you and will bless you, even when you are lonely or afraid? How will you overcome your fears and doubts?

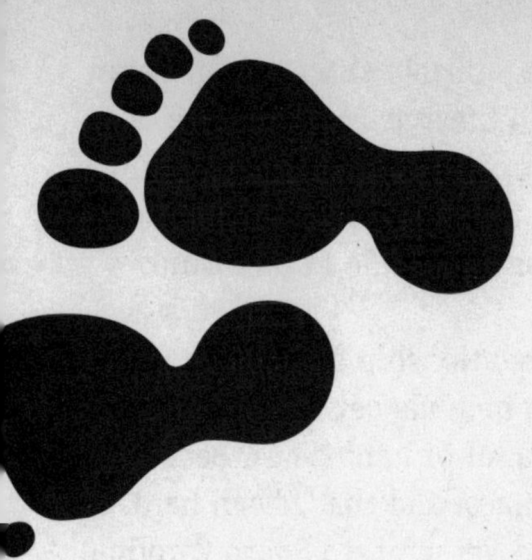

Moving—With My Constant Friend

FOCUSING IN

"You have to have some kind of constant in your life, and for me, that's God."

—William, age 16

Probably the hardest thing for a guy in high school these days is to keep a clear focus. It's a transition time; you're obviously growing up, looking ahead to college and decisions you have to make. Relationships with family, friends, girlfriends. I think that takes a big toll on some people. Just changing relationships, finding out which are good and which aren't. Sports. Just the future in general. There are lots of big decisions. Plus, you've got a lot of peer pressure to do things like drugs and smoking; fitting in is a big part of high school. It can be a stressful time.

I have a very supportive family, though, and I think they've brought me up very well. Since childhood I've been brought up in a Christian family, and that's a big part of our lives. To us, God is Jesus Christ and the Trinity, meaning God the Father; the Holy Spirit, who works in my life; and Jesus, who sacrificed himself to forgive me of my sins. My parents are probably strict by some standards, but it's to encourage a Christian lifestyle. And because of their example, that has become a part of who I am. They do punish me at times, but I think they want it to be a lifestyle that I choose to live, not just a lifestyle they choose for me. So I don't think they're strict in that sense.

I've been encouraged to have a relationship of my own with God, so I've learned to trust in him to help me get through things. And that has helped me get through a lot of hard times. Because of my dad's work, we've moved four times, and that's been hard. I was born in Oregon; then we moved to Vermont, to South Carolina, back to Vermont, and down here to Florida just this past summer. Making those transitions is hard, and they have gotten harder as I've gotten older. In high school I think you are more connected with friends and school; you're more involved in everything.

I had a really close group of friends in Vermont, and I liked the school I was going to. It was a small private school of only about five hundred. I keep in touch with them by phone and e-mail. Actually, my best friend, Jake, moved to Hong Kong while I was still up in Vermont, and this past summer I was able to go visit him. We keep in touch a lot, and we tell each other pretty much everything. He is the person in my life whom I've felt closest to. We can talk about anything. Spiritual struggles like sins, or when we're not seeing in our life what God wants, or it seems like he's just silent up there and does he even exist? Also just daily things that we share together—small things that strengthen a friendship. Girls, definitely. And also we pray for each other. That's a big part. We've been very comfortable in being ourselves around each other, and I think that has put us at a deep level.

I still have a friendship with him. We keep in touch, but knowing that I'm not on that level with anybody now . . . I'm not disappointed, because that was unique. But it has definitely left a hole, and every day I feel it. It has been hard not having those close friends here. I'm optimistic about the future, though. Fortunately, it hasn't been too hard for me to make new friends. It was definitely hard to leave my old ones; it's not so much that *here* is bad, but that *there* was so good.

I think in order to be in a good relationship you have to be confident in yourself. You don't have to try and change who you are to fit the other person's standards, and if it is a true friendship, the other person will accept that. Some people, though, have trouble acting like themselves. Maybe it's from trying to impress the other person, or trying to put themselves ahead of the person. I think everyone to a certain extent wants to elevate himself, and I think that stifles a lot of friendships.

Having a relationship with God is like having the closest friend. I can always talk to God. Some people say that it's not really two-way, but I really do get encouragement knowing that he is caring for me and working in my life, that he actually does orchestrate my life. So it has been comforting. And you know, I can pray to God and know that he loves me as a person and that he will work out his plans for my life. So I can give to him the things that I'm struggling with. I mean, I can plan the future as much as I want, but he's going to make his will happen regardless, so I have to be able to let myself fall back and just trust that he will work things out his way. That takes a lot of courage at times, and it's not easy to do, because as humans we want to hang on to every part of our life and be in control all the time. And you can't be. Moving to Florida this summer felt the most out of control for me, but I had God to fall back on, and he brought me through it.

When I pray to God, at times I may ask him specifically for the health of a family member, or to work out a personal conflict I might be going through with a friend. For college and the future, that he would make those decisions clear. And then just for day-to-day things, like challenging schoolwork. It's not like he's going to throw down a piece of paper with an A+ on it, but he can provide encouragement for me to complete the everyday things as well as the big things.

Not submitting to peer pressure is something I pray about. I have different values—I don't drink or smoke or do drugs—and when I'm with friends who do, it's hard. There's a kind of a wall between the two of us when I say, "No, I'm not going to do that." We can't relate on that issue, which leaves me with mixed feelings. I'm glad that I don't give in to it, but also sad that I can't relate to that friend. In some ways it's almost impossible to get to that most intimate point of a friendship with them, because there's always going to be that difference unless one of us changes. It's hard, because I would like to be closer to that friend, but as far as personal integrity goes, I can't.

The particular sins that challenge me the most are lying or having bad thoughts about other people, but on a big scale, I think that as much as we try, there's no way we can be perfect, because we're sinful. That's hard to deal with; but on the other hand, because Jesus Christ paid for my sins by dying for me, I have been freed from the burden that all of us—Christian or non-Christian—have, of knowing that we are sinful. I think a personal relationship with Christ is the only way to get over sin.

Prayer is how you can have a personal relationship with God, and that doesn't mean you have to stop and bow your head or go to church to pray. You can be thinking of God just as you walk through the halls: "Just help me be able to talk to this person nicely," or "I want to do your will in this decision. Let me know what that is." He doesn't always specifically say something, but a lot of times he'll make a decision clear. And just like a regular friendship, the more trials you go through together, the closer you become. Going through difficult moments in your life in a relationship with God brings you closer to God.

God has helped me deal with the loss of friends and with moving so much. When you move, your whole life is just basically blown away, because if every aspect of your life changes, you have nothing to keep you who you are. You might lose all your values, because there's a barrage of new and different things that are open to you now. You have to have some kind of constant in your life, and for me, that's God. He keeps me together as my whole life changes.

—William Pollack

Young Believer

Young Believer Connection

Check out the character study of Abraham on page 21 of the *Young Believer Bible*. God told him to pack up his stuff and move out of town. God had a new direction for Abraham's life. Because Abraham obeyed, God gave him a whole nation of descendants.

READ: Genesis 12:1-7

Think about It!

What does it mean to you, to have God as a "constant" in your life? Is this true, even when you move?

Estee's Smile

FOCUSING IN

"People who are very old or handicapped can seem frightening."

—Estee, age 11

Estee's mother took her to a convalescent home to visit the residents. So what did they do first? Naturally, they met first with the facility's activity director, who gave ten-year-old Estee oven mitts to put on her hands, clear glasses smeared with a thin coat of Vaseline to place over her eyes, and a sling for one arm. Of course!

The activity director explained that when people get old, or if they are handicapped, certain parts of their bodies don't work as well as they should. For people with arthritis in their hands, reading a magazine is as difficult as trying to turn pages while wearing oven mitts. For those with poor eyesight, their vision is like looking through Vaseline-coated glasses. A stroke can cause a limb to be as useless as an arm in a sling.

People who are very old or handicapped can seem frightening. But Estee began to realize that elderly people and those with handicaps are people just like herself—except their bodies may not always cooperate. She wasn't frightened anymore as she spent the afternoon setting up bowling pins and carrying light bowling balls to the residents in wheelchairs while they bowled.

Months later, Estee attended an art class for kids. Seeing a girl in a wheelchair by herself, Estee sat next to her. "Hi, I'm Estee," she said with a smile.

"I'm Melody," the girl replied and smiled back.

The art class was fun, and Estee and Melody worked well next to one another. When it was time to go home, Melody's mother handed Estee a note that read—

Dear Estee,

Melody and I prayed that Jesus would send a nice girl to say "Hi" to us. And Jesus sent you! Your joyful smile and happy wave made us feel welcome. Many children stare and point fingers at my little Melody. That makes us sad. But your kindness and enthusiasm makes us happy. Thank you very much.

—Melody's mom

—Estee's story, as told by Peggy Sue Wells

Young Believer Connection

Check out the key verse about encouraging words on page 842 of the *Young Believer Bible.*

READ: Proverbs 12:25

Think about It!

Have you ever thought of making friends with someone who is much older than you? Or someone who is handicapped? Think about who in your neighborhood would enjoy talking with you for a while. What could you learn about encouragement?

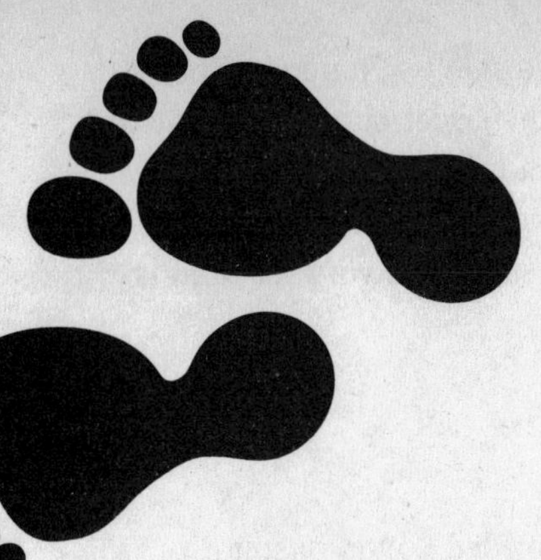

Trying to Ease the Suffering

FOCUSING IN

"I look forward to seeing their smiling faces one day in heaven."

—Alishia, age 16

With sweat beading on my forehead, I walked the eight blocks to see my friend Bunu at the hospital. If ninety-five degrees with 80 percent humidity was their winter in this country called the Congo, I was afraid to even imagine what summer would be like here. Just outside the hospital gate was a small stand where children were selling dried fish from the river just down the way. They yelled something at me in a language I didn't understand; I smiled and replied in the small amount of Katuba that I knew, just enough to greet other people. That sent them scurrying about giggling.

Once I stepped foot on the hospital grounds the entire atmosphere changed. The air was suddenly even thicker than before. A mixture of sounds confused me, with people yelling in Congolese, Katuba, French, German, and whatever other tribal language someone happened to be speaking. Somewhere the men's praise choir was practicing, their melodies mixing with the moans of sick people.

The thing I remember most is the smells. There was the nauseating aroma of salted fish and the sweet odor of the natives' bodies mixing with the moist soil from last night's rain. There was the strong odor of sickness and medicine. It is the most difficult thing to describe, but that particular smell was very real and is still very strong in my mind.

I made my way through the overly crowded Congo hospital, constantly followed by children of all ages, and entered the ward where Bunu stayed. At this hospital the families took charge of feeding and bathing their sick. But she had no family to care for her; starvation had already claimed the lives of her parents.

People might enter the hospital with a broken leg or a gum infection, but without the care of their families, they would starve to death. Starvation was what was happening to Bunu and what had happened to her baby. It was my job to care for them the best that I could while they managed to stay alive, but her little baby had died.

As I walked through the doorway, every person stopped to stare. They all knew me well, since I had been coming eight times a day for the last few weeks. And yet they always greeted me with a look of surprise. Surprise that I had actually returned once more. Surprise that I had not flown back to America to be with my family again. For what was a sixteen-year-old American girl doing in the Congo by herself? And honestly, I had asked myself that same question quite a few times. And yet there I was again.

I greeted everyone the best I could and made my way over to Bunu's bed. I slowly pulled the curtains back, exposing the lady. There was that smell again, the smell of sickness and death. It hits you in the face and as it fills your lungs slowly, heavily.

Yet in some strange way I had grown to love her.

I looked down at her, twenty-six years old, once the mother of a little boy, and I could count every bone in her body. Her legs had contracted so badly that she could no longer walk. Carefully, so not to break her fragile body, I lifted her out of her filthy bed and placed her in a wheelchair. Then with all eyes on us, I slowly pushed her to a small room with a drain in the floor. Once inside the confines of those four walls, with all the dignity that could be allowed in such a situation, I began washing her body as gently as I could. Every bone in her back was visible; I was able to count every rib.

I would then begin the painstaking process of drying her off. No matter how carefully I did things, she would lose skin—a sign of the final stages of starvation. In place of the lost skin were opened wounds. I then returned Bunu to her bed; she was washed, oiled, powdered, and she held on to life with what little strength she had left.

I don't remember much about my walks home at night. I was usually deep in thought. We are told in the Bible that we must love one another as God has loved us. We are not told to love one another when it is convenient or when we get something out of it. We are not told that showing God's love will ever be easy or that when we obey we will be rewarded with all the riches of the world. We are told to love one another as He loves us—completely, wholly, and unconditionally.

For what is physical salvation without spiritual salvation? If I didn't show this lady Christ's unfailing love through my actions, then I might as well have stayed home this summer. If I offered her all the food and riches of the world but never shared with her God's salvation, then what good would I have done?

Watching people die this summer was the hardest thing I have ever done. But I so look forward to seeing their smiling faces one day in heaven and hearing the words that I desperately strive to hear, the words that I live for: "Well done, my beloved. Well done."

—Alishia Gilbert

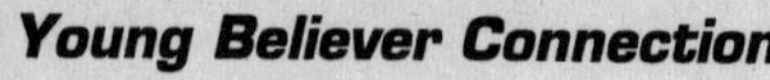

Young Believer Connection

Check out the I Believe statement "God is more powerful than death" on page 908 of the *Young Believer Bible*. Remember that because of Christ's resurrection, all who believe in him will rise from the grave as well.

READ: Isaiah 25:8

Think about It!

Everyone dies, and we must give it some thought, even while we're young. What do you want to be remembered for after you're gone?

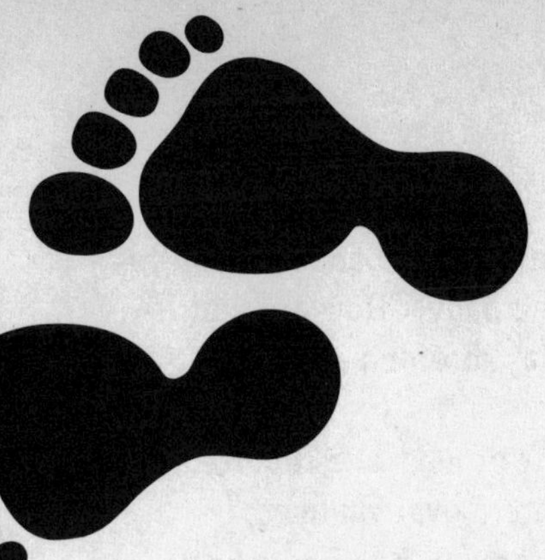

Go Ahead—Pray for Anything

FOCUSING IN

"Those drums were not on my prayer list."

—Josiah's mama

Mama was midway through her eighth pregnancy when nine-year-old Josiah's prayer life changed. Every night the family would gather together to pray before going to bed. Each person, beginning with the youngest, would pray aloud. Daddy was last because he was the oldest, except on the days when he was away on business; then Mama would finish the round.

On this particular night, after three-year-old Hannah had said her prayers, Josiah began his request. "Lord, could I please have a black Lab puppy and a set of drums?"

Mama's eyes popped open and met Daddy's across the room. Though she didn't say anything, obviously the *last* two items on her prayer list would be a black Labrador puppy and a set of drums. Over the next four months, Mama inched toward her due date, and Josiah faithfully prayed the same request for a black Lab puppy and a set of drums . . . every night.

In March, ten-and-a-half pound Lilyanna Faith was warmly welcomed into the family. The following week, Daddy left on his first business trip since the birth of the baby. "How are you doing?" he asked Mama on the Saturday morning after he returned.

"Life is galloping way out in front of me," she reported. "I can't seem to catch it. I feel completely overwhelmed."

"That's understandable, considering you just had a baby, and I was away for a week. I have a handful of errands to run. How about if I take the children with me, and you and Lilyanna take a long nap?" he suggested.

"Great," Mama agreed.

Twenty minutes after the happy band had hit the road, the phone rang. It was Josiah. "Mama, can I keep this black Lab puppy I'm holding? I promise to eat all my vegetables, clean my room, and do my chores."

"Put your father on the phone," Mama said through clenched teeth.

Josiah handed the cell phone to Daddy.

"What are you doing?" Mama asked.

"It's like this," Daddy explained. "We were driving past a farm, and there was a big sign in the yard that said 'Free Puppies.' Knowing how overwhelmed you are feeling, I looked the other way and pretended not to notice the sign. But all the children in the back of the van spotted the sign and got excited. They yelled, 'Look, Dad, free puppies! Black Lab puppies! It's the answer to Josiah's prayers!' So what's a dad to do?"

"What's a dad to do?" Mama echoed. "Put Josiah back on the phone."

"Hi, Mama," Josiah said, hopefully.

"Son," Mama said, "are you going to train this dog so it's a good, obedient dog?"

"Oh, I will," Josiah promised.

"And clean up after the dog?"

"I'll clean up after the dog," Josiah assured.

"I don't need another project, Josiah. I have plenty to do. If you bring this dog home, it will be *your* dog. You must train him and care for him and clean up all his messes. Is that a deal?"

"Yes, Mama, I'll take care of the dog."

"Okay, bring your puppy home. I can't wait to see him."

Josiah named the pup Old Dan after the male puppy in the book *Where the Red Fern Grows.* The following weekend, while Daddy was home with the children, Mama went garage-sale shopping. It was Josiah's turn to have some alone time with Mama, so he scratched Dan good-bye behind his floppy ears and jumped into the passenger seat of the van, and away they went. At the first garage sale they came to, what did they find but a complete set of drums all assembled and ready to play. Mama looked at Josiah. Josiah looked at Mama.

"What's a mom to do?"

Josiah emptied his savings account and proudly brought home his drums. A week later he was playing those garage-sale drums in a fiddle show.

Under Josiah's training, Old Dan went on to become the 4-H grand champion dog in obedience. Mama actually grew fond of the mutt, a free answer to prayer.

"He plays with the children, minds his manners for the most part, barks when someone comes to the house . . . and he talks. It is good to have a male that talks," she said. Indeed, Dan had a singsong way of whining when someone talked to him.

And the drums, well . . . "Those drums were not on my prayer list," Mama said.

—Josiah's story, as told by Peggy Sue Wells

Young Believer Connection

Check out the I Believe statement "God hears and answers prayer" on page 356 of the *Young Believer Bible.* God wants us to talk to him about everything that's on our hearts.

READ: 1 Samuel 1:26-27

Think about It!

Remember all the prayers you've offered to God in your life? How did God answer?

A time he said yes was when . . .
A time he said no was when . . .
A time he said wait was when . . .

What is your prayer today?

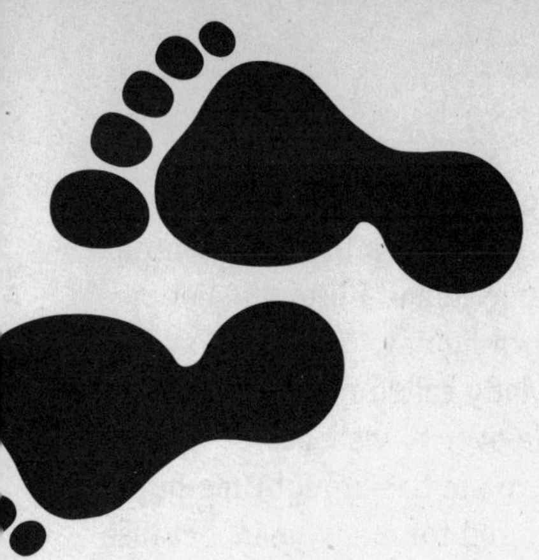

From the Bible: Listen to Those Older Folks!

FOCUSING IN

"This lovely old lady has taught me so much through our talks. . . . I sure hope that I'm just like her when I'm her age."

—Janice, age 17

When I first got my driver's license—*whoa!* Freedom! (Even though my car is a beat-up, rusty old 1985 Chevy Camaro that constantly needs fixing.)

At first I had to share the car with my older brother, Jimmy. Now, because Jimmy is away at Bible college, I've had the car more to myself. Since I felt like a burden asking for a ride to various places, having the ability to go on my own gave me a special opportunity. After driving around by myself for a while, I realized that I could go anywhere and visit anyone I wanted now, without my parents.

So off I drove!

The very first person I visited was an older friend from church who had just spent three weeks in the hospital with a life-threatening infection in her leg. When this lady came home, I brought her some flowers and a card. (I have my own money, too, from my job at a bagel shop.) Later that week this lady called my mother on the phone to thank her for sending me over to visit her.

She told my mom, "Janice's visit to me has brought me hope again in teenagers." This lady had suffered for many years because her own daughter was so rebellious. After hearing this, I prayed for this older friend and became even closer to her. She even told my pastor about our visits.

Next, I visited Grandma, who is an active member of our church. Sometimes we go shopping together, and we've even gone together to various music concerts. She lives by herself since Grandpa died, but I have seen a real difference in her level of happiness since we've been hanging around together.

My mother was very touched by this act of love, and the bond between my mom and me has grown deeper. There's a little problem, though. At times, I've been gone from home on one of my visits longer than my mom or dad thought I should. They always think something has happened to me. Pretty soon, though, they realize that I've done this to serve the Lord. So they have encouraged me to continue in this special ministry. Being a teenager, I tend to make my visits a little more sporadic than planned, but visiting has made me more aware of the needs of others. Then I know how to pray for them better, too.

Anyway, the most memorable person that I have visited over the years was our pastor's mother-in-law, Mrs. Virgie Belcher. I would often sit on the back pew and talk with this special lady when she was visiting from down South. We would chat together about how much things used to cost back when she was a child—like a dime for a gallon of gasoline. Mrs. Belcher could quote Scripture with ease from her long study of the Bible. She would also quote some of the poems she had written late in life. This lovely old lady taught me so much through our talks about the Bible and the One who wrote it.

Once she told me how she had met her future husband. When they first met, he was involved in the local Baptist church as a deacon. However, after they were married, he got upset at some of the men in the church and stopped attending altogether. So Mrs. Belcher raised their children without his going to church—over the next thirty-plus years. She prayed with her children for their dad while being faithful to attend church themselves. Then she realized that perhaps he was not even a Christian. So Mrs. Belcher started praying for his salvation instead of praying for him to come back to church.

When their youngest child, Joan (our pastor's wife), was a senior in high school, Mr. Belcher came downstairs one day and announced that he had become a Christian. He told them he had accepted Christ that past week and was going to go with them to church that morning. This was a huge surprise, and he never did say what events led to his salvation. But after that he was a completely changed person.

Mrs. Belcher would always mention to me that I should not marry until after I graduate from college. And she made me promise her that I would wait in order to date "God's way." Also, she added that God has a husband for me, but that he will not show up until after I graduate from college. Actually, I thought this was cute, and so I promised to do what she said.

I know this is a long and winding story, but it does have a main point, so please keep reading. You see, since Mrs. Belcher lived down South and was able to have an extended visit only at Christmas, last year was my last visit with her at our pastor's home. She had a gift for me: a collection of poems she had written. Soon after, at the age of ninety-three, Mrs. Belcher died. I cried when I heard, although I am certain she is with her Savior, whom she adored, and her husband, too.

Of course, I still visit various people in our church family at Trinity Baptist Church in Taylor, Michigan. But the people I enjoy the most are the older members. Even my mom agrees with me. The other day I said, "Old people are so great, Mom! Don't you think so, too?"

"Yes, they are, Janice. It is nice of you to notice," she laughed. I sure hope that I'm just like her when I'm her age.

—Janice's story, as told by Jillane McGahhey

Young Believer Connection

Check out the character study of Naomi on page 348 of the *Young Believer Bible.* What a lovely elderly lady, who mentored a young girl!

READ: Ruth 1:1-22; 1 Timothy 5:1-2

Think about It!

What is your attitude toward older folks? Think: "One thing I could probably learn from an older person would be . . ." (Fill in the blank!)

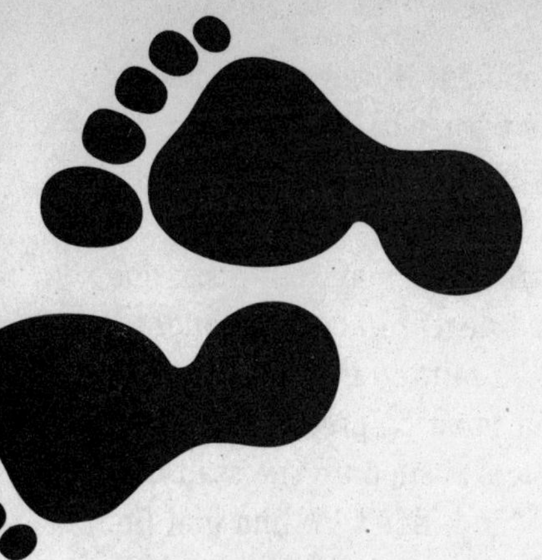

Still My Best Friend—For Always

FOCUSING IN

"You don't realize what you have until it's gone."

—Natalie, age 23

When you're in middle school, your best friends seem to come and go like the waves of the ocean: here today and gone tomorrow. But the memory of those best friends can keep you close no matter how far you separate. Whether the miles or a sudden change of events keep you apart, your memories keep the relationships alive.

This realization came to me at the end of my ninth-grade year. In just one day, everything changed for one of my best friends.

From the day I received that phone call, I have never been the same. It was a day off school, and I was in the process of getting ready to go to Target with my mom and twin sister, Abigail. Just then, the phone rang. On the other line, my good friend Cole seemed to be laughing hysterically.

In the mood for a good laugh, I smiled. However, she began speaking, and I realized that her voice wasn't happy but full of horror and fear. She tried to explain what had happened, but all I can remember hearing is "Jacob" and "drowning."

I didn't know what it meant to drown. It may sound strange, but I never knew that drowning caused death; I always thought it was something that happened when you fainted in a pool. But hearing her shaky voice, I knew that it must be pretty serious. Falling to my knees, I screamed. My mom rushed up the stairs and grabbed the phone. I kept screaming, "God, don't let him die! God, don't let him die!" Then I rushed to the hospital, pajamas and all.

Behind the swinging yellow doors, amid stiff white uniforms in the stark waiting room of the intensive care unit, we began our journey. Little did I realize that the events of May 23, 1996, would show me how fragile life can be.

My friend Jacob's painstaking process to recovery began with a near-drowning accident. Doctors reported that those eight minutes underwater had cut the oxygen to his brain and might leave him as a "vegetable" the rest of his life, meaning he couldn't do anything but breathe.

Quickly I became acquainted with hospital equipment, feeding tubes, seizures, comas, needles, bad news, and more bad news. Special doctors recommended that Jacob be flown to Baylor Medical Center in Dallas to run tests and receive treatment. As time passed, my friend reached what most doctors believed to be impossible—he experienced a miracle and has recovered much better than anyone expected.

Jacob's accident changed my life in ways that were hard to accept. However, I believe I never would have learned these life lessons any other way. In fact, the night before Jacob almost drowned, I wrote in my journal that he had been mean to me. (Remember that I was only in ninth grade.) I was very jealous of my twin sister and his relationship with her. The fact was that he was crazily in love with Abigail. And the fact that she couldn't care less about him was almost too much for me. And here I was, willing to do anything for him to treat me like a friend again.

The night before Jacob's accident, I recall God telling me that Jacob would not always be there for me. I thought this meant he would move away or change schools. It was not until afterward that I even made the connection to his accident. The oddest thing was realizing that in times of trouble, you always go to your best friend to talk. However, my best friend was the one on the hospital bed, with tubes in his nose, and monitors beeping all around him.

As I basically spent all my waking hours in the ICU waiting room, I thought a lot about the meaning of friendship. And I determined for myself that I would remain faithful, no matter what.

It's been three years since that May 23. I've been to Dallas Baylor Medical Center with Jacob three times, spent countless hours (averaging three a day) at the nursing home with him, and spent my lunch breaks with him, not to mention weekend time.

I still go over to his house every day after school and work with him on things like tying his shoes and getting on and off the trampoline. You might see us walking down the road on our afternoon routine of picking up trash. Jacob has an obsession with trash due to an extreme vision problem left over from the accident. He sees better out the sides and beneath his eyes than straight ahead, so all the trash on the curb is in view all the time from the sidewalk and the street.

I can only imagine how humorous it must be to drive by and see a boy walking with arms straight up toward the sky, giddy as a horse running free, and a girl walking behind him, hopelessly holding a trash bag and picking up garbage. However, it doesn't bother me about how funny it looks, because I'm with my best friend. I'm doing things that he really enjoys, just like when we used to skateboard. He used to spend hours with me studying for stupid tests that he needed no help on just so that I could make a good grade. We understood each other, knew each other, and cared for each other in a way that not many teens ever experience. In fact, we've dealt with something that most grown-ups never experience.

You don't realize what you have until it's gone. Through this whole ordeal, I have learned the meaning of true love.

Love gives. That's all.

Time is the greatest thing you could ever give to anyone in life. Anyone can give talents, and most can give money, but when you give of your time, you truly reap the benefits of friendship. I want to close with a story that Jacob wrote about me recently:

> *Natalie is a girl I love. She is beautiful. She is pretty because she has red hair and is tall. She is my friend. She loves God and goes to church. I hope I marry someone who is tall and loves God. I love Natalie. Not because she is my girlfriend, but because she is my friend.*

—Natalie Dowd

Young Believer Connection

Check out the character study of the healed leper on page 1331 of the *Young Believer Bible*. He was truly thankful for the help he received . . . like Jacob was?

READ: Luke 17:11-19

Think about It!

How can you tell who your truest friend is? And what does it mean to *be* a friend? Is it easy or hard?

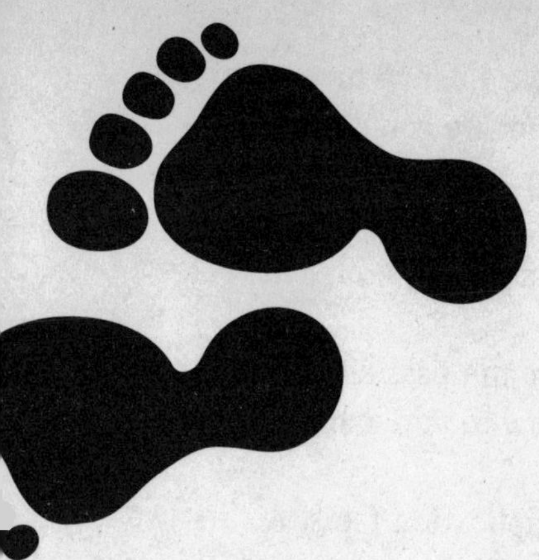

Not Gonna Do It!

FOCUSING IN

"I thought you only bowed before God when you prayed!"
—Haley, age 11

"Mountain, mountain, we're not worthy, Michael, Michael, Michael!" Everyone around me shouted his name, with their knees on the floor and their arms held high in the air. Then they began to bow down, extending their arms to the floor as they said the chant.

The first time this happened I wasn't too sure about it. I really didn't like the whole idea, so when I got on my knees I just stayed there; I didn't bow. I felt very uncomfortable. But everyone else followed our teacher, who bowed before Michael too.

Fifth grade was the first time I had a male teacher. He was very intimidating because he was tall and bald and had a goatee. I also knew about his reputation for being strict. But he wanted us to learn, and he came up with all kinds of ways to reward us.

When we reached certain goals, we'd get to have a party. We earned tokens for doing good deeds that we could spend in a token store. We got tokens for passing our math tests, too. The token store was only open a couple of times a year, and it was a cool little shop where we could buy candy, toys, or school supplies.

One day he told the class, "When you pass all your math tests in a certain period of time, we'll all bow to you and do a chant to honor you." The kids liked the idea.

The math tests covered our multiplication facts. At first we had to do the test in just two minutes. Then, as we got better, our teacher gave us less and less time to complete the test. My classmates thought it was a lot of fun, especially when they were the ones being bowed to and honored.

But I thought you only bowed before God when you prayed! In the Bible, Shadrach, Meshach, and Abednego were willing to die rather than bow before a statue of their king. Deep down I knew this wasn't right.

Many of the kids asked me why I wasn't bowing. They kind of whispered it to me. I told them, "Because I don't bow to anybody but God."

Later, even a few Christian kids came over to ask, "How come you're not doing the chant?" I had the same answer. They told me it was okay because it's just a classroom, and it's just for fun.

Now, I have always attended Vale schools and know all my classmates well. In fact, Vale is a small Oregon town of fewer than two thousand people, so I figured everyone would hear about my behavior in class sooner or later. But I also believed that it would be displeasing to God to bow before a person, regardless of the reason.

I talked to my mom that night about it. "Would you talk to

my teacher, Mom?" I asked. She said she would. But the next day, I knew I was the one who had to talk to him.

I was scared to death.

It was very frightening to go to the teacher because when we did something he didn't like, he made it really clear—in his very loud voice—that he was unhappy.

I went by myself to his desk and told him that I didn't feel right bowing down to people during math. To my surprise, he didn't seem upset at all. Instead, he said, "If there's a problem with your family's beliefs, don't worry about it." I didn't have to bow after all!

Later that day, when the other kids did the chant for a classmate, I sat at my desk and clapped for the top student.

My cousin is another Christian kid and was in my class. He sat at his desk and didn't bow for two of the chants after I had quit bowing. When he didn't bow, I felt glad that someone else was standing up for what he believed.

But after the first two times, he joined the rest of the kids for the chants for the rest of the year. When he went back and started bowing with the other kids, I felt sad, but I didn't discuss it with the other kids.

Soon people stopped noticing me, since we honored a classmate almost every day throughout the rest of the school year. And here's the best part: When I passed my tests my teacher gave me my paper marked with a big red A and a pile of tokens. Only the teacher and I knew about my good grade—nothing more was said or done. I guess he figured out that if I wouldn't bow to the others, I wouldn't want them to bow to me.

But right there, at my desk, I bowed my head in prayer to God. After all, I could not have asked to be excused without His help.

—Haley Markle

Young Believer Connection

Check out the character studies of Shadrach, Meshach, and Abednego on page 1103 of the *Young Believer Bible.* These guys didn't bow, and they didn't burn!

READ: Daniel 3; Romans 14:1–15:4

Think about It!

Think of all the things God considers to be sins. Do any Christian friends disagree with you on some of those things? How do you handle the "gray" areas?

- Things that are obviously sinful:
- Things that are obviously okay:
- Things that I'm just not sure about (the gray areas) . . . :

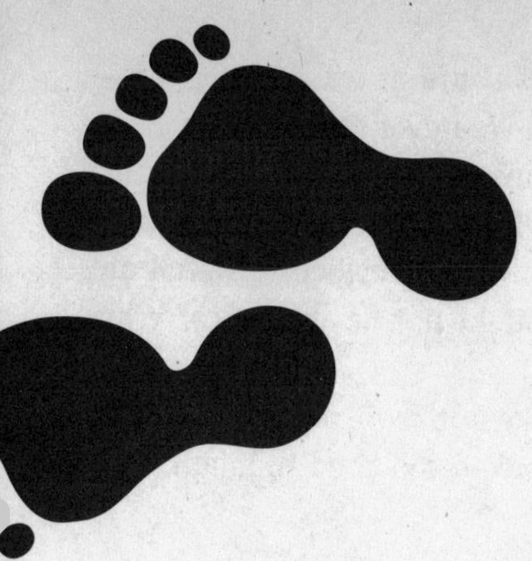

Carry His Load!

FOCUSING IN

"Usually, in tough situations, I make a joke or something. But I was too hot to think."

—Neil, age 13

It was one of the hottest days of the year, probably over a hundred degrees. Richard and I had just finished our first crazy day of middle school, complete with gym class outside in the blazing sun. Then we had to change clothes and stumble from class to class without being sure which way to go. Of course, the seventh and eighth graders were no help, either. We had to figure everything out on our own.

Now came the most dangerous part of our new life as sixth graders. We had to walk about a mile and a half on a very busy main street with other kids pushing their way past us. Just a few feet away, cars flew by us doing fifty miles an hour.

Richard and I shifted our backpacks away from the street as we crammed onto the only sidewalk leading away from the middle school and high school. Hundreds of kids lined the street—some laughing, some pushing, some just trying to get home as fast as possible.

I looked over at my friend to make sure he was okay. It's a habit from back in elementary school. We never talked about it, but he had been really sick once and missed lots of school. When he came back, he'd lost all of his hair from radiation treatments. Some of the kids teased him back then, but I decided to watch out for him. And now he looked as if he might not be able to carry his huge backpack much longer.

Usually in tough situations I make a joke or something. But I was too hot to think, and Richard looked too tired to laugh anyway.

I had brought my Bible to school this day to show some verses to Richard at lunch. We'd known of each other for several years, but now we were in many of the same classes together. So it looked like we could become close friends this year—if we survived!

I wondered to myself how the school expected him to carry all of this stuff home today. Richard's backpack was stuffed with several books, each two inches thick and weighing about five pounds apiece. He couldn't leave them at school, either, because there were no lockers for us.

My pack only held my Bible, since I hadn't gotten my set of math, science, and social studies books yet. So I offered to exchange backpacks on the long walk home.

I really didn't mind. Richard seemed so relieved and had energy to talk all the way to his house without stopping. Then he invited me in to get some water before I walked the two blocks home.

"Hey, you guys look beat!" Richard's dad said as we dropped the backpacks inside his front door.

"Yeah, it's got to be over a hundred, Dad. I wouldn't have made it home without Neil, either. He said we could switch back-packs, since mine was so heavy."

"You mean you have to carry all of those books back and forth to school? Well, I can do better than that. What time do you boys get out of school?"

Before I knew it, Richard's dad had it all figured out. He would pick us up every day right after the last bell. No more walking home from school for us! God really blessed me for helping my new friend that day.

—Neil's story, as told by Rita Medina

YB Young Believer

Young Believer Connection

Check out the I Believe statement "God's love is expressed when believers love and care for each other" on page 384 of the *Young Believer Bible.* David and Jonathan are an example of two great friends who watched out for each other.

READ: 1 Samuel 18:1-3

Think about It!

How do you usually react when you see a friend struggling with a heavy burden?

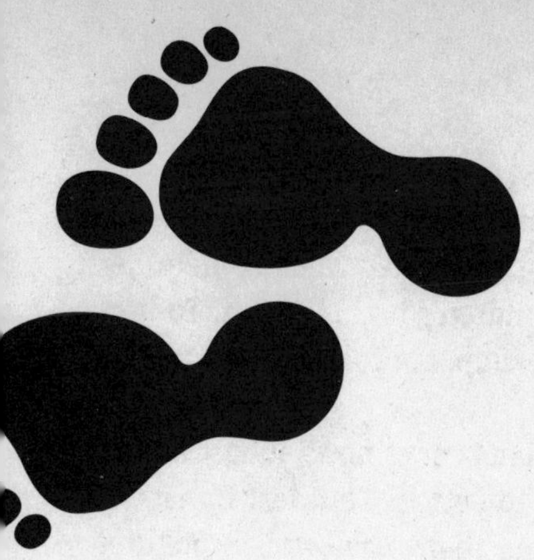

31 More Room—In Nebraska

FOCUSING IN

This year, she has at last found a way to make room in the inn.

—Amanda, age 15

At a white-steepled country church near Tecumseh, Nebraska, a child stood at the pulpit in the dimly lit sanctuary and read, "She gave birth to her first child, a son. She wrapped him snugly in strips of cloth and laid him in a manger, because there was no room for them in the village inn" (Luke 2:7).

In one balcony of the church, fifteen-year-old Amanda Kettelhake listened to the soft echo of the reading against the vaulted ceiling. She had heard these words many times. Every Christmas she pictured the small Christ child lying in the hay and dirt of a stable because no one had made room for him in their home. This year, her thoughts shifted to another child: a three-year-old named Leticia, who lived in the slums of Brazil.

Leticia entered Amanda's life last Christmas . . . as a gift.

Instead of Amanda asking her parents for CDs, clothes, or any of the other items typically on her list, she asked them to help her "adopt" a child through a Christian children's organization. To her surprise, her parents arranged for the support of a little girl in Brazil as Amanda's Christmas gift.

"I wasn't really expecting it," Amanda says now, almost a year from when she first became a sponsor to Leticia, "but last Christmas, I got this box, and I opened it, and there was Leticia's picture right there, and I was like, 'Oh, wow!' I was really excited about it."

Amanda is always busy—in volleyball, softball, swimming, church youth group, and clubs. "Probably too many clubs," she confides. Still, she wants to help other children who are less fortunate.

"This is something I've always wanted to do," she says. "I've loved kids all of my life, and I guess my sponsoring Leticia is God's plan."

She hopes to be a teacher someday and right now is learning a lot from a three-year-old in Brazil. Amanda says her sponsorship of Leticia "sparked an interest" in other cultures and countries. "The night I got her picture," Amanda says with a chuckle, "I was like, 'Oh, Mom, let's go to Brazil now.' She said, 'Well, maybe someday.' I want to go visit sometime. But I don't know how soon that will be."

Amanda receives Leticia's letters after they have been translated into English from Portuguese. "It takes a really long time to get letters back—like four or five months," Amanda says, "but it's really exciting to get them."

Through Leticia's letters, Amanda has learned about Brazilian customs such as celebrating the Carnival holiday with samba parades. "She draws me pictures and stuff," Amanda says, smiling.

In return, Amanda has sent stickers, packs of Kool-Aid, and balloons to Leticia.

"She loves dolls," Amanda says. "I wish I could send some to her, but [the sponsorship organization] has this rule that you can only send things that are flat." Dolls would be too large and would take even longer to deliver.

Leticia is the second of three children. She lives with her parents, two uncles, an aunt, a grandmother, and her brothers in a brick-and-mortar home with a concrete floor. The family's income is twenty-nine dollars a month—less than half of the country's minimum wage. Their combined wages aren't enough to buy the bare necessities of life.

Amanda feels good knowing that the money her parents pay for her to sponsor Leticia helps provide the child with food, clothing, and an education. "It's just a great feeling," she says, "when you get something back from her and you hear how she's doing and all the things she's been up to and how your money has been helping her out."

Amanda says she plans to carry on her sponsorship as long as she can and looks forward to receiving letters written by Leticia herself. "I hope that she knows who I am," she says, "and that we have a really strong friendship."

Amanda refers to Leticia as "my little girl" and keeps a framed photograph of her among the rest of her family photos on a shelf. Leticia is a dark-haired child with cheeks still plump with baby fat and soulful black eyes. Her brows are wrinkled with worry in most of her photographs.

Amanda often thinks about Leticia. At Christmastime, especially, Leticia reminds her of yet another child, one who came into the world as a gift to all. This child grew strong and, filled with goodness as an adult, said, "I assure you, when you did it to one of the least of these my brothers and sisters, you were doing it to me!" (Matthew 25:40).

In the dimly lit sanctuary of her white-steepled church in rural Nebraska, Amanda smiles as the Christmas program draws to a close. This year, she has at last found a way to make room in the inn.

—Amanda's story, as told by Ronica Stromberg

Young Believer Connection

YB Young Believer

Check out the That's a Fact! note on page 1333 of the *Young Believer Bible*. Kids have a special place in Jesus' heart; after all, he came to earth as one. He wants his believers to care for kids—especially the ones who are hungry and hurting.

READ: Luke 18:15-17

Think about It!

When have you felt weak and hungry? Who helped you? Will you do the same for someone else?

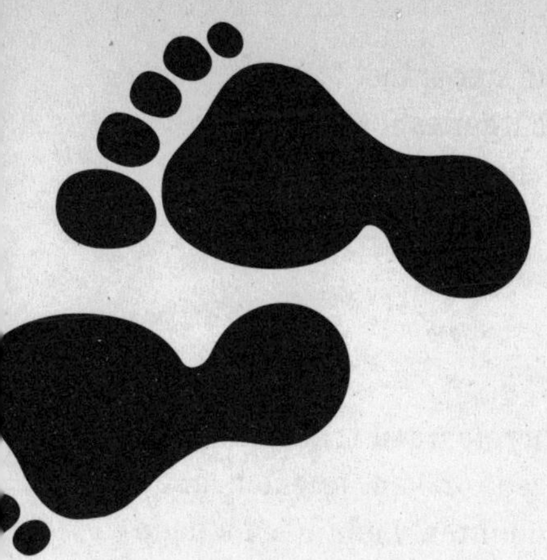

I Can Do All Things through Christ

FOCUSING IN

"Sometimes people don't see me. They only see my wheel-chair."

—Aubree, age 14

Aubree Renae McAnear was born May 25, 1988. Like most Christian girls, she enjoys hanging out with family and friends. She has chores. She's active in church. She sings in her junior high-school choir. She's taken lessons in voice and horseback riding.

Although she's never placed in a competition, she has earned a place on the Lubbock, Texas, Independent School District swim team. After graduation, she plans on attending Belmont University in Nashville, Tennessee, to study music and then pursue a career in Christian music.

Yet she is unlike many other teens in one specific way. Aubree McAnear cannot walk: she was born with spina bifida.

Spina bifida is one of the most devastating birth defects. It happens when the spine doesn't close properly during the mother's first month of pregnancy. Aubree was only four hours old when she had surgery to close the opening in her spine. Over the next six years, she would have eight more surgeries for complications related to spina bifida. She would also be fitted for braces and, eventually, a wheelchair.

When Aubree's parents, Mary and Danny, learned that their unborn baby had spina bifida, they prayed, cried, prayed, researched, and prayed some more. They knew their daughter would need a deep faith in the Lord if she were to live a normal life.

Aubree grew up believing that God could heal her with a whisper, but that it was more important to love Jesus for who he is, not for what he could do for her. Through the years, Aubree's courageous spirit, determination, and faith has touched the lives of doctors, nurses, teachers, friends, and countless strangers.

Aubree never felt she was treated any differently from any other child. With three other active children, Aubree's family was always on the go. When she was little, if her brothers—Keith and Scott—had baseball games, she went too. When her sister, Lisa, had a gymnastic meet, Aubree was there with the rest of the family.

Being a normal kid, Aubree loved playing with her family and friends. When she got her first wheelchair—a cute, hot-pink roadster—her play turned a bit mischievous. On occasion, if her brothers or sister were lying on the floor watching television, she would try to roll over them. If that didn't work, she would back up and try again. She was always getting into trouble like that.

Aubree is happy that her family hasn't "babied" her because of her disability. She likes to do everything for herself and gets upset if she feels like someone is pitying her. "My friends and family are the best. It's like they forget that I'm in a wheelchair, and when I'm with them, I forget it too."

While Aubree's parents have encouraged her independence, they have also realized she will have some limitations. She has often surprised them by going beyond those limitations in her own unique style, however.

As a baby, Aubree would dance with her mother's shoes on her hands. During the fifth grade, she and two other friends performed a hand dance that Aubree had choreographed. It was the hit of the school's talent show. In the sixth-grade talent competition, Aubree sang a song that won third place. She was told that it wasn't necessarily her voice but her showmanship that earned her the prize.

During after-school hours, and on the weekends, Aubree is like any other teenager. She spends the night away from home on a regular basis. Because she has a sweet personality, her friends' parents are happy to have her over, even though it means having to take her wheelchair anywhere they go. Nearly every other weekend, Aubree goes to the movies with friends. She also attends school football and basketball games, and she seems to know everyone in the stands.

Because Aubree went to the same school throughout all her elementary years, it made other kids feel comfortable around her. Everyone knew her and watched her grow up; anything she did was normal for Aubree. This helped others accept her and helped Aubree accept herself. That's not to say that the differences never bothered her. Once in a while, she would say, "Sometimes people don't see me. They only see my wheelchair."

Aubree was six years old when she enrolled in a special aquatics program at the YWCA that allowed for one-on-one training. She loved her coach, Lindol Forbes. He was surprised that Aubree was not afraid of anything. Coach Forbes once told Mrs. McAnear, "I would hate to be the one to tell Aubree that she couldn't do something."

After a year of lessons, Coach Forbes admitted that he

couldn't teach Aubree anything more. She could swim the length of an Olympic-sized pool without stopping. She had incredible lung capacity. However, not everyone believed their eyes when they first saw Aubree in the water. Whenever her family went to a public swimming pool, the lifeguards would jump off their towers and stand at the side of the pool to watch her. After a few minutes, they would slowly back away and climb back onto their towers.

When Aubree entered Mackenzie Junior High, she had few options for her PE credit, and she didn't want to be just a spectator during gym class. Her mother contacted the school district's aquatic office and asked about the swim team. She was told that all kids who wanted to participate had to formally try out for the coaches. She was also told that even though Aubree knew how to swim the breaststroke, she didn't have a chance if she couldn't do the American crawl, also known as the freestyle.

Mrs. McAnear then called the YWCA and found out that not only did they still have the special aquatic program, but Aubree's old coach still taught it. To everyone's amazement, Aubree learned the American crawl in two lessons and reconditioned herself to swimming the length of the pool.

Students from all over the city of Lubbock came to try out for the coveted five spots on the swim team. Six students, including Aubree, were from Mackenzie Junior High. Aubree was the only one from her school to make the final cut. She also went down in the swim team's history—the first kid in a wheelchair to try out and make the Lubbock Independent School District swim team.

Aubree doesn't make a big deal out of being on the swim team. "Swimming gives me exercise and a way to take care of my body."

Aubree McAnear has learned to look—and live—beyond her limitations. "Having spina bifida is difficult sometimes. But, my life's goal is to be a professional singer, and I'm not going to let my disability slow me down. Nothing is going to stop me!" She tells other kids to refuse to limit themselves. "Don't look down on yourself. It won't get you anywhere. If you have self-confidence, you can do anything!"

Aubree can say this because she knows the Lord is her strength. "I thank God for the talents and abilities he has given me. I know that things could be so much worse."

—Aubree's story, as told by Paula K. Parker

Young Believer Connection

Check out the I Believe statement "God has an awesome plan for my life!" on page 42 of the *Young Believer Bible.* God wants to help you succeed in his plans for you.

READ: Genesis 28:15

Think about It!

If you are able to walk, imagine living your life in a wheelchair. How would you want others to act around you?

33 The Quiet One

FOCUSING IN

"Oh, I'm just the curtain guy."

—Andy, age 12

Nobody ever noticed Andy. He was a quiet little kid in my grade at school—not the best one in the class, but not the worst, either. That title belonged to me. He never raised his hand, and once when Ms. Mendez called on him to give an answer, he turned all red and started to cry. She never called on him again.

You might have the idea that Andy never talked to anyone at all, but that's not true. He just didn't like to be the center of attention. He talked to plenty of people one at a time, though, and most of us really liked him.

The day we had tryouts for the play, Andy told me I should go for the lead part. "You'd be good, Pete," he said. "You have the loudest voice, and you do really funny imitations of the teachers. I bet you'd be a great actor."

"No way!" I shot back. "Ms. Mendez hates me. Don't you remember the time she caught me cheating? She told my parents, and I was grounded for a month. And now every time we have a test, she makes it a point to stand right by my desk like I'm a criminal or something. She'd never pick me for the lead."

"She might if you asked her," said Andy. He had this funny look on his face like he knew something.

"Yeah, right." I pulled a straw out of my pocket and shot a spitball clear across the room, hitting Mona on the cheek. She raised her hand to tell, but then the recess bell rang and Andy ran over to talk to her. I ducked out and started a softball game with the rest of the kids.

Right in the middle of the game, when I was up at bat with the bases loaded, Ms. Mendez came stalking out onto the playground, right onto home plate, and put a hand on my shoulder. "Peter, I need to talk to you. Come inside for a minute."

"What did I do?"

"Nothing, yet. But I have big plans for you. Come on, let's go."

From past experience I knew better than to argue with her, so I threw my bat down in the dust a little harder than I should have and followed her into the classroom. Andy and Mona were still there, and Mona looked mad.

"She told you about the spitball, I guess," I said to Ms. Mendez. Mona just rolled her eyes and snapped her gum.

"As a matter of fact, she hasn't mentioned it," said Ms. Mendez, "but you can hand over the straw sticking out of your pocket." I did. "Andy says you're quite an actor, and I think he may be right. I'd like you and Mona to be the leads in the play. Can you sing?"

"Yeah, I guess."

"Can you dance?"

"Never tried. I wanna be a major-league pitcher, not a ballerina."

"See, Ms. Mendez? I told you this will never work," whined Mona.

"Let me hear you sing," said Ms. Mendez. "We'll work on the dancing later."

Not to brag, but I have a pretty good voice and I know a lot of songs from camp. So I blew her away with "When the Saints Come Marching In" and even did all the instruments, pretending I was a trumpet and stuff like that. She loved it. Andy just stood there with a big grin on his face the whole time.

"You're drafted," said Ms. Mendez. "Rehearsals start tomorrow after school."

"What's Andy's part?" I wanted to know.

"Oh, I'm just the curtain guy," he said.

"Nice. No lines to learn."

Andy didn't have an answer for that one; he just smiled.

Over the next two months we rehearsed almost every day until five. Then Andy would follow me home and make me learn my lines, taking all the other parts so I could say mine. It wasn't easy for me. I was great when I could make stuff up on the spot, but memorizing was not my thing. One day I just blew up at him. "Look, you know the whole stupid play by heart already. Why don't you take the lead?"

Andy kind of crumpled and sat down on my front steps. "I can't do what you do," he said. "When you're in front of an audience, a light turns on inside you. With me, I clamp shut like an oyster."

"You should open up a little so people can see what you've got inside," I joked.

"I just can't do it, Pete. That's your job."

That night he invited me to sleep over at his house. I was surprised that my parents let me on a school night, but I think they liked Andy so much better than my other friends that they suspended their usual rules.

After dinner his dad read us a story from the Bible. I wasn't really used to this; at my house we go to church and all, but we don't talk about it much. Anyway, Andy acted like they did this every night of the week and it was no big deal, so I went along with it.

The story was about the disciples Andrew and Peter, which I thought was pretty funny since it was obvious he planned it that way. What was even funnier was that the Andrew and Peter in the Bible were just like us. Andrew wasn't much of a talker, and Peter never shut his mouth. They were brothers, though, and when Andrew met Jesus for the first time, he ran to bring Peter because he knew Peter had what it takes to be a leader.

Andy's dad was cool about the story. He didn't preach this big lesson to us; he just told the story and let it sink in. As it turned out, I guess I was the one who preached the lesson. But that's the way I am, always running off at the mouth.

"So if it wasn't for Andrew running to get his big-mouth brother, Peter wouldn't have even been one of the disciples. The church would have been pretty different!" I said.

"It would indeed," said Andy's dad. And that's all he said. I could see where Andy got his quietness.

A week later was opening night, and thanks to Andy I was ready. I have to admit I loved being in the spotlight, even when I had to dance with Mona. Andy only had to prompt me once when I missed a cue. He prompted other kids, too, mostly because I couldn't resist ad-libbing a little, and that would throw them off. But the audience loved it, and we got a standing ovation at the end.

At the last curtain call, Andy handed me the flowers I had to give to Ms. Mendez. I took center stage and gave my speech about the people we had to thank, and Ms. Mendez kissed me on the cheek. I could have done without that. Then I had a brainstorm.

"There's someone else I have to thank," I told the audience. "He worked just as hard as anybody, especially with me, and if we missed a line, he's the one who'd get us back on track. If it wasn't for him, Ms. Mendez never would've let me on the stage." I glanced at her to see if she was mad, but she was just nodding and smiling. After all, it was true. I motioned to Andy to come out from behind the curtain, but he just stood there shaking his head frantically with a look of panic in his eyes. I knew I'd made a mistake.

"My friend is really shy and wouldn't want me to say his name," I continued, "but I just want him to know that if it wasn't for him, I'd be sitting up in the balcony shooting spitballs instead of standing here in the spotlight making this speech. Thanks, dude."

I saw Andy's dad in the audience take out a handkerchief and wipe his eyes. A lot of other people did the same. Ms. Mendez burst into tears and threw her arms around me. Ordinarily I would have wriggled away from her, but I was a little teary myself. The whole thing would have ended like a tragedy instead of a comedy if Andy hadn't lowered the curtain so I could quit while I was ahead. Once again, he made me look real good.

I'll never forget my friend Andy. I won't pretend he made me into a model student; I still had my share of trouble and ended up in the office every now and then because of my big mouth. But he would always put in a good word for me, like "Let Pete organize the field day—the kids'll listen to him." I started getting involved in school activities on my own, without Andy nudging me, because it was fun to be in charge.

We lost track of each other after sixth grade because his family moved away, but every once in a while when I get too full of myself, I step back and remember good old Andy behind the curtain, feeding everybody their lines. I could never be like that; I need the applause. But Andy could never be like me either.

It takes all kinds.

—Andy and Pete's story, as told by Nancy Massand

Young Believer Connection

Check out the character study of Peter on page 1255 and the story of the first disciples on page 1349 of the *Young Believer Bible.*

READ: Matthew 26; John 1:35-42

Think about It!

Are you outgoing or shy? How can you tell? (For extra thought: Do you believe God uses both kinds of personalities?)

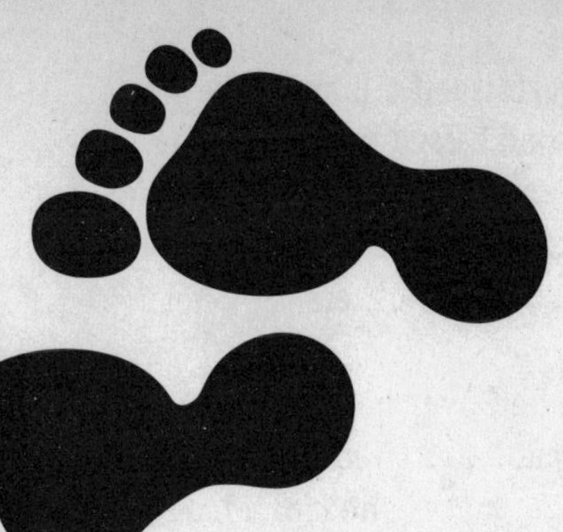

34 The Baby-Sitter's Club

FOCUSING IN

"You see, I'm really organized, and . . . well, I know a lot of people."

—Annalisa, age 17

The alarm went off at 6:15 A.M. Annalisa groaned and hit the "snooze" button, her mind still in a fog. Then her eyes flashed open. *It's Wednesday!* she realized. Annalisa flung back the covers, a slow grin spreading across her sleepy face.

Getting up early on Wednesdays was rough but worth it. Ever since her friends from church had started meeting for breakfast once a week, Annalisa looked forward to Wednesdays more than any other day.

Right in the middle of her busy week, she could spend time with her Christian brothers and sisters. They worked through lessons of a Bible study every day on their own and then compared notes at the Wednesday breakfasts. They also prayed with each other. It was the most important part of Annalisa's week. It helped her focus on her priorities in life—and the group encouraged her to grow as a Christian.

For example, everyone else in the group seemed to be doing

something great for God. Annie had performed a piano solo in a youth symphony orchestra, Elizabeth had raised money to buy gifts for children at the battered women's shelter, and Laura had served on the missions committee at their church and was always helping others. Annalisa wanted to be like the others, but her schedule was already packed.

As hot water from the shower rushed over her head, she began to rehearse her "to do" list. It made her tired just thinking about it. *How did I get myself into such a mess?* she sighed.

Quickly she finished up and slipped back down the hall to dress. She threw her books in her backpack, hoping she wasn't forgetting something. But that rarely happened. If there was one thing she was good at, it was being organized. *I wonder if I can use that ability to do something great for God?* Other people used their talents to serve Him. Well, maybe when she got older. Maybe when she graduated from high school and had more time . . .

She jumped into the car and drove to the restaurant. Most of the girls were already there, including her youth director, Sarah. Usually everyone smiled and greeted her, but today they just sat there.

Annalisa slid into their booth. She looked around. Annie stared at her mug of hot chocolate and frowned. Elizabeth watched Sarah mournfully. And Sarah looked like she had been crying. Laura quietly leaned forward and met Annalisa's puzzled gaze.

"Mrs. Hoffman died," Laura began.

"Mrs. Hoffman?" she said, trying to place the name with a person.

"You know little Marin at church, and her new baby brother, Cole?" Laura said. "Their mom died."

Annalisa held her breath for a moment and then leaned hard on the table. It couldn't be possible. Mrs. Hoffman? She wasn't even thirty years old. What about Cole and Marin? Mrs. Hoffman's son was only one month old, and his sister, Marin, had just turned two. Annalisa could picture them in the nursery at church. She remembered their dad bringing them in—a tall, smiling guy who adored his children and treasured his wife.

"She had a heart condition when she was a little girl," Sarah explained. "Nobody thought she could still have complications from it, but she did. That's how she died. They're not really sure why." Elizabeth put her arm around Sarah's shoulders.

"But what is Mr. Hoffman going to do now?" Annalisa asked. She still couldn't believe it.

"Well, he's going to need a lot of help," Sarah said. "He's a single dad now, with two little kids. It's gonna be a lot of hard work to run his business and take care of his kids. Our church family's gonna need to be a big part of his life."

The girls kept quiet for a while, pondering this sad problem. They ate a solemn breakfast and tried to talk about their Bible study for a little bit. But it was hard to concentrate.

Just before they got up to leave for school, Annalisa spoke up. "I wonder if we could baby-sit for him sometimes?" she said. "We wouldn't charge him or anything. We could just be . . . older sisters for Marin and Cole!" The other girls nodded with enthusiasm. Sarah smiled and put her arm around Annalisa.

"I'm sure he would love that," she said. "Keep thinking about it, and we'll put together a plan."

Annalisa began to pray. She prayed all through that week—all through the memorial service and worship the next Sunday. Every time she thought about Marin and Cole, she paused and prayed. And slowly, slowly, an idea began to form in her head. It seemed nearly impossible to fit in her schedule, but somehow that just didn't matter. She would make the time. She would tell Sarah when the timing was right.

Finally, Annalisa found her chance. At the end of worship one Sunday, she saw Sarah with Mr. Hoffman, standing at the back of the church. Little Cole was in a stroller, gurgling away. Sarah looked her way and smiled.

Annalisa took a breath and approached her friend. "Sarah, I have an idea," she said. "Do you think Mr. Hoffman still needs baby-sitters? I want to organize that for him."

Sarah's eyes widened. "Of course!" she said. "But let's ask him."

"Mr. Hoffman?" Annalisa asked.

The young father turned around. He had a sadness in his eyes that made Annalisa wince.

"This is Annalisa," Sarah said, motioning toward her. Doug Hoffman shook Annalisa's hand. "She's wondering if you still need baby-sitters."

"Of course!" he said, nodding.

"Well, Mr. Hoffman, I was thinking . . . I mean, if you needed it I could put together a list of students from church who could baby-sit for you, and then when you needed someone you could call me." Annalisa took another deep breath. "We wouldn't charge you or anything, because Marin and Cole are . . . well, we're like big sisters and brothers to them. And we'd love to spend time with them. Even if you just need someone to watch them while you do stuff around the house."

Mr. Hoffman's face brightened. Sarah grinned from ear to ear.

"The Baby-Sitter's Club!" she said. Annalisa smiled, gaining confidence.

"You see, I'm really organized, and . . . well, I know a lot of people. All you would have to do is call me, and I'll call around till I find someone who can do it. Would that work out for you? What about this Saturday?"

Mr. Hoffman stuttered. Cole gurgled in his stroller, smiling up at his dad.

"Wow. I don't know what to say," Mr. Hoffman said. He

seemed truly shocked. "I . . . well, yeah, Saturday would be great. I mean . . . you don't mind not getting paid? I'd be happy to—"

Sarah politely cut him off. "Oh, no. This is her ministry to you. Annalisa, why don't you line someone up for this Saturday and then give Mr. Hoffman a call?"

Annalisa almost jumped for joy. She said good-bye to them, knowing that she had finally found the great thing she could do for God.

—Annalisa's story, as told by Sarah Arthur

YB Young Believer

Young Believer Connection

Check out the I Believe statement "The Holy Spirit gives power to believers so they can serve him" on page 61 of the *Young Believer Bible.* God gives each one of us special talents and wants us to use them for him.

READ: Genesis 41:38-39

Think about It!

Have you ever had the opportunity to help someone through a really tough time? How did you feel knowing you were helping to ease their hurts?

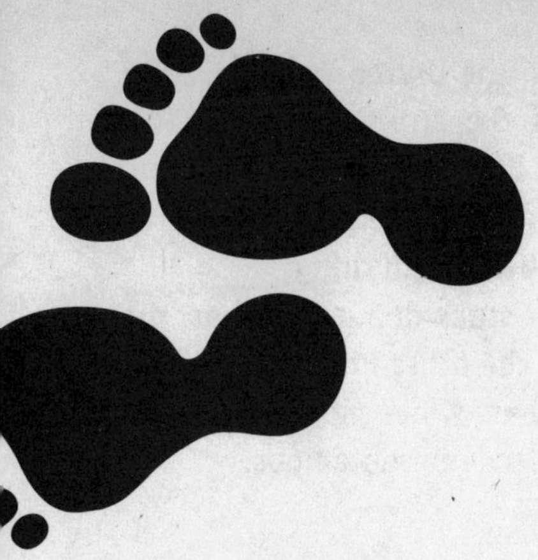

One Bagel—To Go

FOCUSING IN

"You don't usually see people begging in our part of the world. But I sure recognized the look on [that man's] face."

—Julie, age 12

The man standing on the street corner looked tired and dirty. In his right hand, he held a small piece of cardboard that he used as a sign displaying "Will Work for Food."

I saw the man's face as our family drove by on the way to our favorite bagel place. I didn't know him. We live in a small Pennsylvania town, and people usually know one another around here. So I guessed that he was homeless—maybe he'd come from Philadelphia, about forty miles away.

You don't usually see people begging in our part of the world. But I sure recognized the look on his face. I remembered the faces of the people that we met on a mission trip to Ecuador. Some people's eyes had a glazed stare that showed how numb and hopeless they felt on the inside. But here was a person in need right in my own neighborhood!

I've usually been with people from our church when I've offered to help others like him. Besides our mission trip to Ecuador, we've taken five more trips within the United States, mostly doing manual labor for people in need. Some of the kids on the trip would help out with the Vacation Bible School that our group presents to the people, but I always ended up helping the adults with manual labor, not talking about God or anything.

When I've asked why I always get stuck doing the labor, the church leaders said that I encouraged the other kids so much when I sang silly songs and told stories to them while we worked and painted at the job site. I guess my attitude is contagious.

When we got to the bagel place for breakfast, I asked my mom if she saw the guy with the sign. It turns out that she wanted to help him too. My dad tried to think of some outside jobs that we could offer to him, like maybe shoveling snow or something. But we really didn't have any work for him.

I thought that he must really be in need, because he was willing to work to get some food. He wasn't just begging for money.

When the waitress came over to take our order, I said that I wasn't very hungry. I didn't feel like pigging out anymore after I saw the man. So when it came my turn to order, I asked for a toasted bagel with cream cheese—to go.

I'm usually a little grumpy in the mornings anyway, so my mom didn't give me a hard time about not eating. By the time our food came to the table, the discussion had changed to what we wanted to do the rest of the weekend. But I didn't say much. I had a plan, and now I had to figure out how to get my family to go along with me.

As my family walked back to the car, I finally spoke up. "Could we drive back home the same way we came? I want to see if that man is still standing on the corner."

My dad and mom smiled and said, "Sure, Julie," and we pulled out of the parking lot and headed back home. My heart pounded as we got close to the corner where the man had been standing. Would he still be there? We'd been in the bagel shop for an hour! Would my parents go along with me? I prayed that God would give me the courage to do what I had to do.

"There he is, Dad. Stop the car!" I said. Dad seemed surprised, but he turned the corner and pulled the car into a parking space. I jumped out of the car and walked over to the man with the sign.

"Here. It's a bagel with cream cheese," I said as I handed him the bag.

The man smiled and reached out to shake my hand and said, "Well . . . God bless you. My name's Tony."

Then he took my breakfast and put it away in his backpack to enjoy later. I excused myself and jumped back into the warmth of our family car. Everyone waved to him as we pulled away and headed back home. Tony stood there with his hands up in the air and his eyes closed. He looked like he was thanking God for the food.

Mission accomplished!

That night I prayed for the man again, and told God how happy I was that he would use me to help someone else in need. Here is what I wrote in my journal that night.

February 19

Dear God,

Thank you so much for the experience with Tony. I can't stop thinking and praying about him. It's so amazing the way you work in such strange and mysterious ways. I never would have thought he could be a blessing to me, but he was when he started praying about the plain bagel and cream cheese, and thanking you (I guess) with his hands upturned to you. Please help me to never forget that memory—and, if possible, to come in contact with him again.

You are so marvelous and special, God!

Love, Julie

P.S. Please help me to be more grateful for my food. I learned that lesson from Tony!

—Julie Desch

Young Believer Connection

Check out the Can You Believe It? note on page 100 of the *Young Believer Bible.* God provided food each day for the Israelites—even dropping it from heaven for them! Sometimes God takes care of us in unexpected ways.

READ: Exodus 16:1-18

Think about It!

Have you ever complained about being "starved"? Were you really?

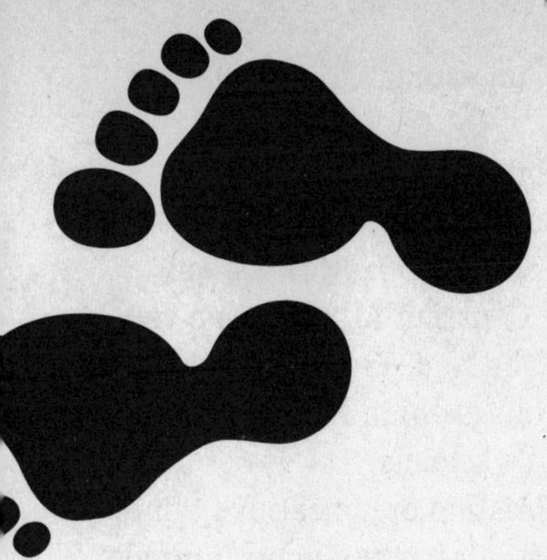

Fellowship's Goal Is Victory off the Field

FOCUSING IN

"I had a big head when it came to track because I won the state last year."

—Courtney, age 17

The Fellowship of Christian Athletes means many things to participants. To Ashley George, it is "the most impacting and rewarding thing that I've done." To Courtney Johnson, it has been a lesson in humility. It has taught Jay Peck "to be open about your life with God." But to all three students, the fellowship has been a winner.

Founded in 1954 by a small group of athletes, the fellowship had its first national camp two years later in Colorado. It has seen steady growth in the last two years in central Ohio, where groups known as "huddles" operate mostly in high schools. Huddle meetings for prayer and discussion are held weekly at the schools. In 2000, there were sixty-five huddles in central Ohio high schools; today there are more than a hundred. The regional attendance total—including athletes, coaches, and non-athletes—has climbed from twenty-eight hundred in 2000 to an estimated six thousand this school year.

Tim Brown, the fellowship's Columbus metro area director, said many high school students are looking for something different, and that Christianity can be that something. "How we get them there is to use the Fellowship of Christian Athletes as a vehicle to introduce them to Jesus Christ," he said. Brown has been concentrating on developing huddles in area high schools, and eventually he will do the same in middle schools.

College students involved with Christian organizations typically join other ones such as Athletes in Action or Campus Crusade for Christ. The fellowship, however, has huddles at Ohio Wesleyan University in Delaware and Muskingum College in New Concord, according to Brown. High school huddles partner with a nearby church, which often has a staff member assist the group.

The Rev. Keith Bradley, associate pastor at Columbus Christian Center on the Northeast Side, has worked with students at Mifflin, Beechcroft, and Brookhaven high schools. He said the fellowship gives them "an opportunity to actually stimulate their focus on something bigger than themselves."

"They're really dealing with a lot of immoral temptations," he said. "Kids have a whole lot to distract them from dreams, goals, and vision and discipline."

At Brookhaven, participation has grown to about sixty. Marv Whiting, the group's huddle leader and a teacher and coach, said many students who come from difficult home lives often feel alone. The fellowship can help, he said. "It shows them first of all that there are other kids just like them who are dealing with the issue daily," Whiting said. "But they also need to know they can call on the Lord.

"In a lot of cases, they're able to find that they have something they can hold on to, and if it's not a physical person, then maybe it's a spiritual person." While a teacher is assigned to each huddle, all meetings are student led. The groups are permitted to meet at schools during nonclass time, such as lunch hours.

For students, the fellowship can be inspiring. Ashley George, who participated at Westerville North before graduating in 2002, said being with her peers has motivated her. "You're seeing that you don't have to follow conformity and that there are moral people out there who are willing to fight for what they believe. . . . It's just really encouraging to be surrounded by a group of people like that," she said.

George, who was a swimmer and tennis player at North, is a freshman at Ohio State University and attends a weekly meeting sponsored there by Campus Crusade for Christ, and Athletes in Action. She has stayed involved with the fellowship and was a leader at a fall retreat.

Athletes can make a difference in schools because they are often looked up to, she said, and they need to recognize that their talents are God-given. "When we're blessed in that way, we need to stand up for that and share why we are blessed and give credit where credit is due," George said.

Johnson, a Brookhaven senior, became involved with the fellowship last school year and, with Peck, is a student leader this year. Last spring, she was a state champion hurdler on the track team. The fellowship helped put things in perspective. "I had a big head when it came to track because I won the state last year. . . . It makes you humble. With God, you understand that you can't do everything on your own. It made me realize that he's helped me through a lot of stuff," Johnson said.

The fellowship also takes on community projects, and the Brookhaven huddle recently helped collect coats for needy kids. Johnson said she hopes the group can begin working with homeless shelters.

Peck, a senior who played football and is on the track team, said the fellowship has taught him "to be humble when things aren't going your way." He said speakers who attend meetings have something worthwhile to offer. "When they talk to you and talk about their life and talk about what they went through, you sort of really feel it," he said.

But students aren't the only ones who get something valuable from the fellowship. Whiting said he is involved in part because, as a Christian, he believes he should look for ways to help others. But there is more. "The other thing it does," Whiting said, "is that during those meetings, I just have such a great feeling. I know that what's being said is helping somebody. I know that. And it just gives me such a great feeling. It is a spiritual event for me."

—Courtney's story, as told by Dennis M. Mahoney

YB Young Believer

Young Believer Connection

Check out the Can You Believe It? note about the first Bible studies on page 290 of the *Young Believer Bible*. Bible studies have been around for a long time. Obviously they're important!

READ: Joshua 8:34-35

Think about It!

How important is it for you to stay in contact with other Christians (for prayer and Bible study)? Can you really live for the Lord all by yourself?

By Dennis M. Mahoney, in *The Columbus Dispatch,* 10 January 2003 (Friday, Home Final Edition. Section: News, Faith & Values, pg. 01E). Used with permission.

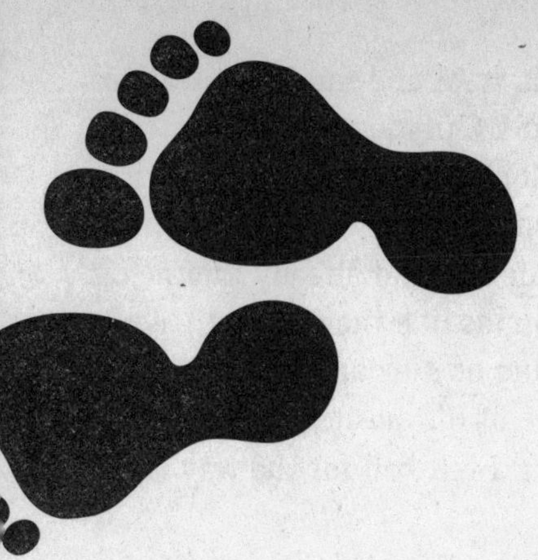

Just Trying to Learn

FOCUSING IN

"They teased Alex just because he was trying to learn the things he didn't know yet."

—Billy, age 11

"Hey, Dad," Billy called as he came in and took off his jacket. Dad was sitting on a stool at a counter between the kitchen and living room.

Dad looked up from the book he was reading. "Hi, Billy. I figured you'd be back from the pizza place sooner. Is everything okay?"

"I stayed longer with Alex after the other guys left."

"He's the one who just became a believer in Christ, right?"

"Yes, Dad. We get along really well. We have a lot of things in common. Except . . ."

"Except what, Son?"

"Well, today Alex was asking some questions, and some of the other guys made fun of him. They teased Alex just because he was trying to learn the things he didn't know yet. Then they all left after saying they didn't know why I wanted to stay there with Alex."

Billy paused. Dad got up from his stool and sat down next to Billy to listen. "Alex didn't grow up in a Christian home, Dad. The others have. Alex was given up for adoption as a baby, and until he was six, he lived in a lot of different homes."

"So, some of the guys thought Alex should already know things they were taught long ago? Sounds like they should have been more understanding and accepting of Alex and his questions. You stayed afterwards to explain some of his questions, then?"

"Well, yes, and to encourage him. I felt bad for the way they acted."

"I'm proud of you, Billy. You did the right thing."

The next day, Billy, Alex, and the other kids went to the winter youth event planned at the church. People formed groups and played games for points. Some games were about the Bible, and some were just fun games of skill. Alex was excellent at shooting free-throw baskets. Everyone cheered him on, and he made more baskets in two minutes than anyone else. Alex also helped the group in the scavenger hunt, which required a lot of math skills to be able to figure out the clues placed in spots around the church.

John asked, "Hey, Alex, where did you learn to shoot baskets like that?"

"When I was staying in California at a foster home, my foster brother Eric taught me. He loved basketball."

Curt added, "You are really good at math, too. We wouldn't have won the scavenger hunt without your help."

Alex smiled.

Just then the youth pastor, Tim, stood and said a few words. "I'm glad everyone has had so much fun. I'm also glad we've made it through the night without breaking anything." Pastor Tim smiled. Some of the kids laughed.

"I am glad to see that many of you have brought friends. There are a lot of faces I have not seen. I know there are also some new believers here with us today. Be sure to encourage them.

"You all know my first name is Timothy. I know a lot of you call me Tim, but I have always liked being named after the one Paul taught and mentored in the Bible. Paul was older and wiser, and Timothy was a young man with a lot of questions. Yet Paul was patient with him. He was always encouraging him. Timothy became a good leader because Paul was willing to be patient with him.

"Paul said we should accept each other whether we are new believers or have known God for a long time, just as Christ accepted us. He said whether weak or strong, we are welcome. After all, where else can you learn to become strong?

"I hope that we all follow Paul's example of patience and encouragement. Well, it looks like the food is ready. Since we have already asked God's blessing and given thanks, you can begin to line up.

"Enjoy, and don't forget to save some for me."

The other guys around the table looked at Alex. Jimmy spoke first. "I think we did break something. We probably really hurt you yesterday when we made fun of your questions, Alex. I'm sorry."

Curt agreed. "I'm sorry, too. I'll try to help from now on."

John smiled and said, "I guess there are some things we can learn from you, too!" The other guys agreed. Then they all ran over to the line for the food.

On the way, John shouted, "Hey, Alex, do you think you could help me with my math homework?"

"I think so," Alex yelled back. "But not until after we eat!"

—Billy and Alex's story, as told by Peter D. Mallett

Young Believer Connection

Check out the character study of Timothy on page 1559 of the *Young Believer Bible.* He was ready to learn about the Christian life as his friend Paul patiently taught and encouraged him.

READ: 1 Timothy 1:18-19; 6:11-21

Think about It!

What kinds of encouraging things can kids say to each other in tough times? Make a list of the possibilities.

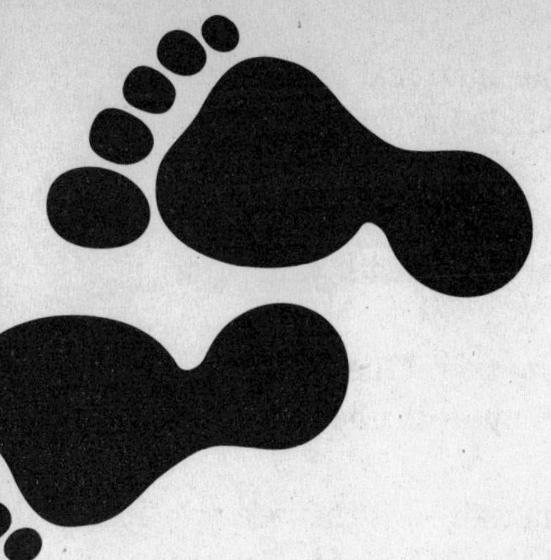

God Will Make a Way

FOCUSING IN

"God took what seemed like a frustrating dead end and turned it into a highway."

—Tim

The school year started like any other for Tim. But it would soon become very different. It all began at the small diner where the Breakfast Club met Wednesday mornings. Breakfast Club was the only thing that could get Tim up earlier than he needed to be. Not only did it mean good food, but it also meant being with other Christian teens from his school.

Tim bit into his egg sandwich.

"Did you pray about 'See You at the Pole'?" the leader of the club asked him.

Tim froze mid-bite. Gooey yolk slid down his chin. He did pray about it. He was hoping she would forget to ask.

"Well?"

"I guess God wants me to lead the prayer."

"You guess?"

"Well, he does."

It's not that Tim didn't think he could do it. Every year he participated in the "See You at the Pole" national prayer event at his school. But leading prayer was a whole lot harder than just being there.

The leader smiled. Tim knew that smile. It was the kind of face that said, "God's going to do great things with you." Tim hoped he could live up to the honor.

"Tomorrow I'll make a poster," Tim said. "Then I'll get the vice principal to sign it and put copies up in the hallways." It should have been an easy task.

In the office a few days later, Tim waited as the vice principal read the poster. "So this is all about prayer?" he said. "I'm new here. I'm not sure what the policy is on an event like this. I'll give you an answer tomorrow."

The vice principal dropped the poster into a "To Do" basket. It rested on top of a looming pile of papers. Leaving the office, Tim didn't worry, because they put up posters every year. Someone would tell the vice principal it was okay.

The next morning Tim peeked into the office. "Is the poster ready?" he asked.

The vice principal pulled it out from the middle of an even higher "To Do" pile and put it on the desk. "Now it's on the top of the list," he told Tim. "I'm going to double-check with the Board of Education. As soon as I hear anything, I'll tell you."

Every day Tim showed up at the office and, each time, he left without the signed poster. Tim began to wonder whether this was God's will after all. Maybe he should just give up and let the kids who already knew about it show up on their own at the pole. Part of him thought that was enough, but another part said to keep doing everything he could, even when it seemed useless.

A week before SYATP, Tim told the Breakfast Club, "I can't get approval to put up the posters."

"But how are we going to let everyone know about it?" one kid asked.

"We could just tell people," another suggested. Sure they could, but would anyone remember?

"I think we'd better pray," Tim said.

Days later, no poster approval came. The Board of Education dragged its feet. Tim thought they were waiting for the event to pass. "If only we could hand out the posters," one of the kids said. "Can we?" The reply came back from the vice principal. They could—outside the school, with no special signature. With just one day left, the Breakfast Club members armed themselves with hundreds of fliers. Every kid who stepped out of the bus received a flier. Was it enough? Was it too late?

With the Breakfast Club hard at work getting the word out, Tim needed to get ready. Even if only a few students showed up, he would lead the prayer. That much he knew.

He searched through the Scriptures, jotting down his thoughts as he went. Praying that he chose the right things to say. He didn't know when he went to sleep that night what would happen the next day. A big question hung over the SYATP prayer.

At Breakfast Club early that morning, the question loomed. And the question stayed when he arrived at the school, half asleep, with butterflies fluttering freely in his stomach. But then, as the members approached the pole, as the small group from the club surrounded him, and as others began to gather like iron filings to a magnet, the question mark evaporated. Tim found himself encircled by more than ninety students. Tim had expected a small, loyal group to show up, but God revealed a greater plan. God had taken what seemed like a frustrating dead end and turned it into a highway.

Now it was time to pray. Tim raised his Bible. The crowd around the pole fell silent. Some girls a few yards away, who were arguing about which diet drink tasted best, fell silent. The boys knocking each other's books out of their hands fell silent. The group passing by stopped and fell silent. Something grabbed their attention. Then Tim heard the sound of his own voice reading and explaining Scripture. When he began to pray for the school, for the administration, and for all of America, the crowd, bowing their heads, let God into their midst. Some girls began to cry. They were not Breakfast Club girls, but God was touching them anyway.

Was Tim supposed to lead the prayer that year? Yes. Did it matter that he was not sure right up to the last minute if it would all work out? No. It didn't matter, because God had all the details under control. All Tim needed was to do his part, in faith. God took care of the rest.

—Tim's story, as told by Clare Cartagena

YB Young Believer

Young Believer Connection

Check out the character study of Moses on page 79 of the *Young Believer Bible.* Moses was shy and sometimes afraid. And when he was leading his people away from Egyptian slavery, he, too, ran into a "dead end"—the Red Sea. But he kept going, by faith.

READ: Exodus 14:5-31

Think about It!

What is the hardest part about moving ahead by faith when the outcome is unclear? When have you trusted God this way?

Ready for more?

Other items available in the Young Believer product line:

Young Believer 365

Be sure to check out
www.youngbeliever.com

Never stop believing!

365?? You mean every day??
You'd better believe it!

Maybe you know something about the Bible . . . or maybe you don't. Maybe you know what Christians believe . . . or maybe it's new to you. It's impossible to know everything about the Bible and Christianity because God always has more to show us in his Word. *Young Believer 365* is a great way to learn more about who God is and what he's all about.

Through stories, Scripture verses, and ideas for how to live out your faith, this book will help you grow as a young believer. Experience God's power each day as you learn more about God's amazing love, his awesome plans, and his incredible promises for you.

Start today. See what God has in store for you!

COMING SOON

Watch for the Young Believer fiction series coming Spring 2004!

o to www.youngbeliever.com for updates.